HUCKLEBERRY HANNAH'S

COUNTRY
COOKING
S A M P L E R

BY DEANNA HANSEN-DOYING

ILLUSTRATIONS AND DESIGN
BY TIM ACOSTA

This book is dedicated to my husband Jack who tirelessly supports, motivates and endures me.

To my dear friend Ruth, who reminds me so much of Emily, and with whom I, too, carry on a long distance friendship.

And to my Lord Jesus Christ who walks with me on the good days and carries me through the tough ones.

ISBN #1-56044-050-3
Library of Congress Catalog Number 90-81714

Cover Design and Illustrations by Tim Acosta
Graphic Design and Computer Layout by Bryan and Danette Blair

Montana Country Samplers
P.O. BOX 664
Eureka, MT 59917

Manufactured in the United States of America
First printing April 1990

The Goodies!

This book was designed for "chocolate junkies", "midnight refrigerator raiders", and anyone who figures life can be "fixed" by applying sweets and snacks liberally.

I am convinced that what people really want are great, gooey, "totally indecent" desserts, snacks, and goodies that are easy to prepare, and wonderful to eat. It's just a fact of life. So here they are...dozens of them.

When I researched the recipes for this book I made it a point to use only the very best ingredients and so should you! After all, you deserve the best. Every recipe is a sure thing, though with a little imagination, I know you could make them even better. So get up out of that chair, tuck this book under your arm, and march into the kitchen. Start creating all the magnificent goodies you always knew you could. Have a ball! I'll be thinking of you.

The Story

Emily Jane Bennette, born July 6, 1886, was a delicate child with strawberry blond hair and green eyes. She had a reserved and gentle nature, for the most part, but also a considerable stubborn streak if provoked. Her hair was stylish, her clothes were tasteful, and her posture was perfect. And though seemingly the perfect little lady, Emily could run like the wind, eat berries by the handful and had a distinctive giggle that was terribly inappropriate. In 1902, Emily went away to college at her parents' insistence. During her two years at college she met Franklin W. Sawyer, the son of a clockmaker. She came home to Montana in 1904, married Franklin in March 1908, and returned to South Carolina to be the wife of a clockmaker, at the age of 22.

Hannah Marie Markuson, born November 12, 1886, was a dark haired, dark eyed girl full of life and mischief. Always the defender of everything and everyone weaker than herself, Hannah could usually be found in a slightly rumpled dress, a hair style that was more functional than becoming, and an infectious smile that made everyone she met adore her. She liked to laugh and be the center of attention, which of course, was not becoming of a young lady in her day. This did not seem to bother Hannah either in her childhood or as an adult. She believed that everyone should be their own person...and indeed she was. Hannah married Andrew David Hansen, a local rancher, in June 1903, at the age of 16, and began a new life as wife and mother.

Emily and Hannah grew up together in Montana....Emily in "town" and Hannah on "a ranch". As different as night and day, they met, as most children do, in school. The two girls were inseparable. Hannah, the gregarious, boisterous child, found mischief and childhood adventure at every turn. Emily timidly followed along, most of the time worrying more about the consequences of their actions than enjoying the splendor of the moment. The two girls laughed and played their way through childhood, confided their deepest secrets and most vulnerable feelings through adolescence, and shared the tears and joys of adulthood.

In 1909 both young married women, separated for what appeared to be forever, began a "long distance" friendship through letters that lasted over 38 years.

CONTENTS

METRIC COPE CHART

VOLUME	WEIGHT	OVEN TEMP.
1/4 tsp. = 1 ml.	1 oz. = 30 g.	250 F = 120 C
1/2 tsp. = 2 ml.	2 oz. = 55 g.	275 F = 140 C
1 tsp. = 5 ml.	3 oz. = 85 g.	300 F = 150 C
1 tbl. = 15 ml.	4 oz. = 115 g.	325 F = 160 C
1/4 cup = 50 ml.	5 oz. = 140 g.	350 F = 180 C
1/3 cup = 75 ml.	6 oz. = 170 g.	375 F = 190 C
1/2 cup = 125 ml.	7 oz. = 200 g.	400 F = 200 C
2/3 cup = 150 ml.	8 oz. = 250 g.	425 F = 220 C
3/4 cup = 175 ml.	16 oz. = 500 g.	450 F = 230 C
1 cup = 250 ml.	32 oz = 1000 g.	475 F = 240 C
		500 F = 260 C

EMERGENCY SUBSTITUTIONS:

1 1/2 tsp. cornstarch = 1 tbl. flour

1 whole egg = 2 egg yolks plus 1 tbl. water

1 cup fresh milk = 1/2 cup evaporated milk plus 1/2 cup water
OR 1 cup reconstituted nonfat dry milk plus 2 tbl. butter

1 oz. unsweetened chocolate = 3 tbl. cocoa plus 1 tbl. shortening

1 cup honey = 1 1/4 cups sugar plus 1/4 cup liquid

EQUIVALENT MEASURES

3 teaspoons = 1 tablespoon
4 tablespoons = 1/4 cup
5 1/3 tablespoons = 1/3 cup
8 tablespoons = 1/2 cup
10 2/3 tablespoons = 2/3 cup
12 tablespoons = 3/4 cup
16 tablespoons = 1 cup
1/2 cup = 1 gill
2 cups = 1 pint
4 cups = 1 quart
2 pints = 1 quart

4 quarts = 1 gallon
8 quarts = 1 peck
4 pecks = 1 bushel
1 oz. liquid = 2 tbl.
16 ounces = 1 pound
32 ounces = 1 quart
8 oz. liquid = 1 cup
1 oz. liquid = 2 tablespoons

BREADS
BISCUITS
&
MUFFINS

BREAD TALK

Making bread is fast becoming a lost art. Homemade bread cooling on the kitchen counter is one of the most comforting sights I can imagine and can be a part of every cozy kitchen. I find baking bread a relaxing and satisfying way to spend an afternoon, and it is much easier than most people expect. The key to great bread, as with all baking, is TLC. Use the best ingredients, warm surroundings, and patience. Bread will not be rushed. Have a wonderful time. Remember to serve bread FRESH or freeze as soon as cooled.

BISCUIT TALK

Unlike breads, biscuit dough should be "handled" as little as possible. Ingredients should be lightly stirred just to moisten mixture....never beaten to blend. Bake biscuits just to golden brown to insure a light, fluffy, and moist texture. Be sure to serve them hot....right out of the oven.

MUFFIN TALK

As you use these wonderful muffin recipes, remember that muffins seem hearty but should be handled with care. An under cooked muffin is soggy and gooey, while an overcooked muffin has the consistency of cardboard. Test muffins, as you would a cake, by inserting a tooth pick. In addition, muffin batter should be lightly mixed...never beaten...to insure rich texture. Oh, and one last thing. Muffins freeze and re-heat beautifully!

NOTES

Hannah's Sunbeam Bread

Makes 2 large loaves or 2 doz. rolls
(Light, semi-sweet, and moist)

2 tbl. dry yeast
1/4 cup lukewarm water
1/2 tsp. sugar

Dissolve together and set aside to activate.

1/3 cup sugar
1 cup powdered milk (dry)
2 cups warm water
1/2 cup shortening
1 tsp. salt
3 eggs (slightly beaten)
4-5 cups flour
Butter

Combine shortening, water, milk, sugar, and salt. Stir to melt and dissolve all ingredients. Add eggs. Stir to blend. Add 2 cups flour. Stir. Add yeast mixture. Stir. Add 2 more cups flour and stir to blend lightly. Turn out onto floured board and knead lightly until dough is no longer sticky to the touch but not dry. Return to bowl. Cover and set in warm (not hot) place to rise. When twice its original size, form into loaves or rolls. Place in baking pans as applicable. Let rise again to twice its size. Bake at 350 degrees. 10-15 minutes for rolls....30-40 minutes for loaves (or until golden brown). Turn out of pans immediately. Brush tops with butter. Place loaves on their sides (rolls on cooling rack). Cool. Serve fresh or freeze.

Everybody should have a dog and a cat. A dog to adore them, and a cat to ignore them.

April 4, 1909

My dearest Hannah,

I promised to write just as soon as we were settled. And though we are just barely that, I couldn't wait to send you a complete accounting of our new home here in South Carolina. Hannah, it is simply the lovliest house! Franklin must have driven himself mad looking for just the perfect residence. I won't bore you with all the details, but I will tell you that we have a beautiful veranda complete with a swing! It is just like the one you and I used to spend summer afternoons in, at Mamma's, when we were girls. I'm sure Franklin had it installed especially for me so I wouldn't feel so homesick. All Franklin's family has been so very kind and helpful .... truly making every effort to make me feel at home and to help me adjust. (I use the term "all family" loosely, since

Franklin's eldest sister, Leona, is just as nasty to me as ever. What I ever did to deserve her, I will never know. God loves her too, I guess. Give me strength!

I do miss Montana so! Make no mistake, I'm thrilled to live in such a beautiful city as Columbia, but just the same, change is never easy. Especially for someone like me. In defense of South Carolina, I will say that spring comes much earlier here, and the flowers are in bloom everywhere. Sometimes the fragrance is simply overwhelming and the colors, Hannah.... It's all as beautiful as I remembered. I'm sure I will grow to love it here, though Montana will always be my home...and you my dearest friend.

Franklin's business is located very near to the college where we met. I can hardly believe that it was almost seven years

Emily's Buttermilk Braid

Makes 1 large braid
(rich, golden bread)

2 tbl. dry yeast
1/4 cup lukewarm water
1/2 tsp. sugar

Dissolve together and set aside to activate.

2 cups buttermilk
2 1/2 tsp. salt
4-6 cups flour
1/4 cup butter (melted)
1 egg beaten with 3 tbl. milk

Combine buttermilk, salt, and butter. Add yeast mixture. Add flour 1 cup at a time, until batter is thick and sticky. Turn out dough onto floured board. Knead until firm and smooth, but not dry. Return to bowl and let rise in warm area until twice its size. Punch down and divide into 5 sections. Roll each piece into 2 1/2 foot length. Lay side by side and pinch top ends together. Number ropes from left to right. Braid rope 2 over 3, then 5 over 4, 3, and 2. Then rope 1 over 2 and 3. Repeat until braid is formed. Pinch bottom ends together and tuck both top and bottom ends under braid. Place braid on lightly greased cookie sheet, cover and let stand 15 minutes. Bake at 375 degrees until golden brown (about 30 minutes). Brush with egg and milk mixture. Cool and serve fresh or freeze.

If you want things to run smoothly on the sea of matrimony, don't sail into him every time he's late for dinner.

ago. I was such a child then. I can still remember how self-conscious I was when I was near him. Imagine anyone ever being nervous around that sweet gentle soul, but everything seemed to embarrass me then. I suppose I haven't changed all that much, but after all, I'll be 22 in July and you would think I would out-grow all that nonsense and be more sophisticated. Anyway, I'm off the subject. What I meant to say before I started prattling, was that Franklin's shop is just wonderful and perfect for a clockmaker.... not as big, of course, as his father's shop was, but perfect nonetheless. Franklin is so talented that I'm sure he will be a huge success.

Speaking of prattling, here I have been going on about me and haven't even bothered to thank you for the wonderful quilt you made us for our wedding present. Hannah, you

Crusty Cottage Bread

Makes one oval loaf (thick chewy crust)

2 tbl. dry yeast
1/4 cup lukewarm water
1/2 tsp. sugar

Dissolve together and set aside to activate.

4 cups flour
2 tsp. sugar
2 tsp. salt
1/2 cup dry powdered milk
2 cups warm water

Mix together sugar, water, milk, and salt. Add yeast mixture. Stir to blend. Add flour until mixture is thick and sticky. Knead on floured board until no longer sticky, but not dry. Return to bowl and let rise until twice its size. Punch mixture down and remove from bowl. Form into rounded oval loaf. Place on lightly greased cookie sheet. Make several very shallow slashes on top of bread with knife. Cover and let rise 20 minutes. Bake at 425 degrees for 30 minutes. Reduce heat to 350 degrees and bake an additional 10 minutes. Cool. Serve fresh or freeze.

Basic Whole Wheat Bread

Makes 2 loaves (hearty and full bodied)

2 tbl. dry yeast
1/4 cup lukewarm water
1/2 tsp. sugar

Dissolve together and set aside to activate.

1/2 cup shortening
2 cups hot water
1 cup dry powdered milk
2 tsp. salt
1/2 cup brown sugar
2 cups whole wheat flour
2-3 cups white flour

simply amaze me! Just when I think you are the biggest oaf of a girl, you surprise me with an intricate piece of work like this. The Prussian blue in the quilt matches exactly the flowered print of my bedroom draperies. Thank you, dear. I will cherish it forever. As a matter of fact, I have been spending a considerable amount of afternoon time "under" it recently. I just don't seem to have alot of energy as of late. Probably just the change in climate.

I will close for now. Give my love to Andrew and the girls. Doesn't Mary Ella have a birthday in April? The 16th, and she will be 4, as I recall. Give her a special hug and kiss from her "Auntie Em".
Missing you.
Emily Bennette Sawyer
(have been just dying to sign my new name)

Combine shortening, water, sugar, milk, and salt together and stir to dissolve and melt ingredients. Cool to lukewarm. Add whole wheat flour. Stir. Add yeast mixture and stir to blend. Add white flour 1 cup at a time until dough is thick and sticky. Knead in remaining flour until dough is no longer sticky, but not dry. Return to bowl, cover, and place in warm place to rise. Dough will double in volume. Punch down. Form into loaves and place in well greased loaf pans. Cover and let rise again. Bake at 350 degrees for 40-50 minutes or until well browned. Brush with butter. Remove from pans and cool loaves on their sides. Serve fresh or freeze.

Oatmeal Farm Bread

Makes 2 loaves (great with soup)

2 tbl. dry yeast
1/4 cup lukewarm water
1/2 tsp. sugar

Dissolve together and set aside to activate.

2 cups boiling water
1 1/4 cups quick oats
1/2 cup molasses
1/4 cup brown sugar
1/2 cup vegetable oil
1 tsp. salt
4 cups white flour
2 cups whole wheat flour (fine ground)
3 eggs (beaten)

Combine water, molasses, sugar, oil, and salt. Stir to dissolve sugar. Cool to lukewarm. Add 2 cups white flour and eggs. Stir to blend. Add yeast mixture. Stir. Add whole wheat flour. Stir to blend. Knead in remaining flour until dough is smooth, but not dry. Oil dough lightly. Return to bowl, cover and chill 2 hours. Divide into loaves and place in well greased loaf pans. Cover and let rise in warm place until doubled in bulk. Bake at 350 degrees until well browned, about 50 minutes. Brush tops with butter. Remove from pans and cool loaves on their sides. Serve fresh or freeze.

Remember ..... The end doesn't always justify the jeans.

Montana Black Bread & Vanilla Butter

Makes 2 loaves (a hearty, mellow winner!)

Bread:
2 tbl. dry yeast
1/4 cup lukewarm water
1/2 tsp. sugar

Dissolve together and set aside to activate.

1 oz. unsweetened chocolate
1 tbl. butter
1 1/2 cups water
1/4 cup dark molasses
2 tbl. cider vinegar
1 tsp. salt
1/2 cup wheat germ or all bran
2-3 cups flour
1 cup rye flour
1/2 cup buckwheat flour

Melt chocolate, butter, water, and molasses together over low heat. Add vinegar, salt, and wheat germ. Let stand 15 minutes until lukewarm. Add yeast mixture. Add buckwheat and rye flour. Stir to blend. Add white flour 1 cup at a time until mixture is thick and sticky. Knead in remaining flour until dough is smooth, but not dry. Return to bowl, cover and place in warm area until dough rises to double in volume. Punch down and form into loaves. Place loaves in well greased loaf pans. Cover and let rise to

September 11, 1909
Dear Emily,

So you are finally pregnant! I know you hate that word, but pregnant is exactly what you are and saying you are "expecting" is a bit silly, isn't it? Expecting what? That it will snow...that the mail will arrive by 1:00... WHAT? Honestly, Emily, sometimes you are just plain dim. I'm so glad that I live on a ranch where life is just life. Well I certainly didn't mean to write and throttle you. Sorry. At any rate, you are going to be a mother in December. I'm thrilled for you, Em. After all, I must thoroughly believe in motherhood since I have three of my own. As you always remind me...three in five years! I just don't know what happened. (Well I DO, but explaining it would really make your lip twitch.) Guess I'm just meant to have lots of youngsters around. My

double volume once again. Bake at 375 degrees for 45 minutes or until well browned. Brush with butter. Turn loaves out of pans onto their sides. Cool and serve with vanilla butter.

Vanilla Butter:
1 lb. butter
1/2 cup powdered sugar
1 tbl. vanilla

Whip butter until very fluffy and pale. Gradually add powdered sugar. Beat until smooth and creamy. Add vanilla. Serve at room temperature or chill. Do not allow to warm before serving.

Home Sweet Home Rye Bread

Makes 2 loaves (rich and mellow)

2 tbl. dry yeast
1/4 cup lukewarm water
1/2 tsp. sugar

Dissolve together and set aside to activate.

1/2 cup shortening
2 cups hot water
1/2 cup brown sugar
1/3 cup molasses
2 tsp. salt
2 cups rye flour
3-4 cups white flour

Combine water, sugar, molasses, salt, and shortening. Stir to melt and blend ingredients. Cool to lukewarm. Add rye flour and yeast mixture. Stir to blend. Add white flour, one cup at a time, until mixture is soft and sticky. Knead in remaining flour until dough is smooth and firm. Return to bowl, cover, and place in warm place to rise double its size.

sister, Abby, is "expecting" too. She wrote that her baby is due in June. This is her first as well. It looks like the two of you are in the same boat, you might say. I'm glad it's you and Abby... and not me. No more babies for me! I'm only 23 and it seems as though I have been "expecting" forever. I feel like my maternity clothes should be called "eternity" clothes. You realize that Babe is 5, Mary Ella is 4, and Beth is nearly 2? Andrew loves having babies around, as do I, but enough! The ranch alone represents more work than I can accomplish. Andrew agrees with me, but I know in his heart that he wishes he had a son.....makes me feel so guilty.

I cannot believe that you are married! Or for that matter, that either of us are. What happened to our childhood, and all the fun we had together? I

Punch down. Form into loaves and place in well greased loaf pans. Cover and let rise once again to double in volume. Bake at 375 degrees for 30 minutes or until well browned. Remove from pans and turn loaves onto their sides. Cool. Serve fresh or freeze.

Old-Fashioned Sourdough Bread & Starter

Makes 3-4 loaves (Do not make this bread when you are in a hurry....it's time consuming...but it's worth it!)

Starter is made and kept forever or until you choose not to have it any more. You simply keep adding to this mixture every time you make bread. Impossible, you say? I have known people who have sourdough starter that is over 20 years old! Ready? Let's make sourdough!

2 cups flour
1/2 tsp. dry yeast
3 tbl. sugar
2 cups warm water
1 tsp. salt

In a medium sized crock, stir all ingredients together to make a smooth paste. Put lid on and set in warm place to "sour". Stir several times a day for 3 days. At the end of the third day, place mixture in refrigerator. The day before you wish to make your bread, follow the directions for "the night before".

The Night Before: (thought I was kidding, didn't you.)

2 cups warm water
1 tsp. sugar
1/2 tsp. salt
2 cups flour

suppose I never imagined that we would ever be separated, and now you are so far away. I feel absolutely amputated. Am I ever going to see you again? And what is this "Emily Bennette Sawyer" business? Aren't you the smug one. You with your lovely musical name and me stuck with "Hannah Hansen". Sounds remarkably like the squeak and hiss of a broken wheel, doesn't it? I could have kept my maiden name, too, you know. But Hannah Markuson Hansen would really have been a handle. Guess I'll just leave the fancy names to fancy ladies like you.

What a beautiful Indian summer we are having. Andrew took all his girls for a picnic down by Sutter's Pond after church last Sunday. Pastor Burkey's "stopping to smell the roses sermon" must have gotten to him.

Add all ingredients to your starter and stir vigorously until smooth. Let stand at room temperature overnight. The next morning, put 2 cups of this mixture back into your refrigerator to preserve your starter for the next time.

Making the bread: (Whew! Finally.)

2 cups starter
1 tsp. salt
2 cups warm water
3 tbl. oil
1/2 cup sugar
6 cups flour
1 egg beaten with 2 tbl. milk

Combine starter, salt, warm water, oil, sugar, and 2 cups flour together in large bowl. Stir to smooth and blend. Knead in remaining flour. Cover and let rise to double volume. Knead again and form into long slender loaves. Place on lightly greased cookie sheet (one loaf per sheet). Cover and let rise again. Bake at 375 degrees for 45 minutes or until golden brown. Brush with egg and milk mixture. Serve warm. Yum!

One good turn gets all the covers.

At any rate, we all had a wonderful time. All except Mary Ella, that is. Babe pushed her into the water, of course. I don't understand where a beautiful little girl like Babe got such a nasty streak! She is always picking on somebody. I just know the Lord gave her to me to teach me patience.

Goodbye for now, sweet Emily. My love to Franklin and his family.....even Leona.
Love, Hannah

Whole Wheat Irish Soda Bread

Makes 1 Round Loaf
(bake this "biscuit like" bread in a cast iron skillet)

2 cups white flour
1 cup whole wheat flour
3/4 cup sugar
1 tsp. baking powder
1 1/2 tsp. salt
1 tsp. baking soda
2 cups buttermilk
3/4 cup raisins
1/3 cup butter (melted)
2 eggs (beaten)
1 tbl. caraway seeds
1 tbl. sesame seeds
2 tbl. butter (melted)

Mix first 6 ingredients together. Add buttermilk, raisins, 1/3 cup butter, eggs, and seeds. Stir to blend. Line the bottom of a 10 inch cast iron skillet with wax paper. Grease paper. Pour batter into skillet and smooth evenly. Baste dough with remaining butter. Bake at 350 degrees until golden brown (about 1 hour). Cut into wedges and serve warm.

Down Home Buttermilk Biscuits

Makes 1 doz. (an all time favorite)

3 cups flour
1 tbl. baking powder
1 tbl. baking soda
1/4 tsp. salt
3/4 cup butter (softened)
1 1/2 cups buttermilk

Combine dry ingredients. Cut in butter. Add wet ingredients. Stir lightly, just to blend. Roll out dough 1/2 inch thick onto floured board. Cut into rounds with 2-3 inch diameter drinking glass. Place on cookie sheet and bake at 425 degrees for 15-20 minutes or until just barely golden.

9

Note: For tasty variations.......add 1 1/2 cups sharp cheddar cheese or 1/2 cup frozen (unthawed) blueberries!

If you want to feel guilty....call your mother.

Easy English Muffins

Makes 18

5-6 cups flour
3 tbl. sugar
2 1/2 tsp. salt
1 package dry yeast
1 1/2 cups milk
1/2 cup water
3 tbl. butter

Combine 2 cups flour, sugar, salt, and yeast in large bowl. Stir to blend. In saucepan, heat milk, water and butter. Cool to lukewarm. Pour milk mixture over flour mixture. Beat well. Gradually stir in enough flour to make a soft dough. Knead dough on well floured surface adding flour until dough is smooth and firm, but not dry. Form into ball and brush with vegetable oil. Place dough in bowl. Cover and let rise until double in bulk. Roll out dough 1/2 inch thick and cut into 3 inch diameter rounds. Roll tops in cornmeal. Place on cookie sheet, cornmeal sides up. Cover and let rise again. Fry muffins, cornmeal sides down, for 5-6 minutes at medium heat until golden brown. Turn muffins, and repeat. Cool and store in air tight container.

If you are such a good cook...Why do we have to pray before every meal?

Pizza Dough

Makes 2 pounds

2 tbl. dry yeast
4 tbl. warm water
1 tsp. sugar

Dissolve together and set aside to activate.

4-5 cups flour
5 tbl. olive oil
1 tsp. salt

Combine 4 cups flour, oil, and salt. Add yeast mixture. Stir to blend. Knead dough, adding flour as needed, to make dough firm and smooth. Cover and let dough rise until double in volume. Use dough immediately for delicious pizzas or divide in thirds and freeze until ready to use.

If you wait too long to marry your dream boat, you may find that his cargo has shifted.

Lemon Tea Bread

Makes 1 loaf (delicate)

1 cup sugar
1/2 cup milk
1 stick butter
3 eggs
2 cups flour
1 1/4 tsp. baking powder
1/4 tsp. salt
2 tbl. lemon juice
1/2 tbl. grated lemon rind

Combine sugar, milk, eggs, lemon juice, and butter. Beat 1 minute. Add dry ingredients and grated peel. Stir to blend. Grease and flour 9 X 5 inch loaf pan. Pour in batter. Bake at 350 degrees for 1 hour or until golden. Cool and remove from pan. Glaze.

January 5, 1910
Dear Hannah,

    She is a little dark haired, green eyed angel. Or at least that is how Franklin describes her to everyone who will listen. She was born December 30th just before midnight in a very easy birth. Honestly, Franklin's sisters had filled me with such horror stories that I was truly terrified, but all went remarkably well. We named her Julianna Leona. Julianna after Franklin's grandmother, which pleases me since Grandma Sawyer is such a dear old soul. And Leona after you know who. I was going to protest but discretion is the better part of valor you know. Julianna is the best baby, Hannah, and so beautiful. She doesn't look anything like my side of the family, thank goodness. I was so afraid that she would inherit the Bennette strawberry hair! She does have my green eyes though,

Lemon Tea Bread (cont.)

Glaze:
1 cup powdered sugar
1/4 cup lemon juice

Mix together until smooth. (Add a little warm water to thin if necessary.) Pour over bread.

Spiced Apple Bread

Makes 1 loaf

1 cup milk
1/2 tsp. cider vinegar
1 tsp. lemon juice
1 stick butter (softened)
1 cup brown sugar
2 eggs
1 tsp. vanilla
2 tsp. baking soda
1 tsp. cinnamon
1/2 tsp. allspice
1/4 tsp. salt
2 cups grated apples (peeled)

Combine milk, vinegar, and lemon juice. Let stand 10 minutes. Combine eggs, sugar, butter, and vanilla. Beat 1 minute. Add milk mixture and blend. Add dry ingredients. Stir to blend. Add apples. Stir. Pour batter into well greased and floured loaf pan. Bake at 350 degrees for 45 minutes or until bread tests done. Cool and remove from pan.

When the cat's away .... there is less hair on the furniture.

and I am just vain enough to be ungraciously proud.

Speaking of being proud, Franklin is the worst. He can't keep his hands off her. Carries her with him everywhere when he is home. He holds her by the hour in the rocker next to the fire, whistling away while he rocks. I'm sure you well remember Franklin's off key whistle. I'm frightened to death he will make her tone deaf. But I think she understands him better than anyone. She simply smiles and gurgles in spite of that annoying noise he makes.

No other big news to report. I will write again soon.
Love, Emily

Banana Nut Bread

Makes 1 loaf

1 cup sugar
1/2 cup shortening
3 very ripe mashed bananas
1/2 cup chopped nuts
2 eggs
2 1/2 cups flour
1 tsp. soda
1/8 tsp. salt

Combine sugar, shortening, bananas, and eggs. Add dry ingredients and nuts and mix well. Pour into well greased and floured loaf pan. Bake at 350 degrees for 45 minutes or until bread tests done. Cool and remove from pan. Serve.

Carrot-Zucchini Bread

Makes 1 loaf

1 1/2 cups vegetable oil
2 cups sugar
4 eggs
3 cups flour
1 tsp. soda
2 tsp. baking powder
1/4 tsp. salt
1 cup grated carrot
1 cup grated zucchini
1/2 cup chopped nuts

Mix oil and sugar. Beat in eggs. Add dry ingredients. Stir to blend. Fold in nuts, carrots and zucchini. Pour into 2 well greased and floured loaf pans. Bake at 350 degrees for 30 minutes or until bread tests done. Cool. Remove from pans. Glaze.

Glaze:
1/4 cup orange juice concentrate
1/4 cup sugar

Cook ingredients over low heat. Bring to boil. Cool slightly. Pour over bread.

Any time a child is seen but not heard ..... don't wake him!

Granny's Gingerbread
Makes 1 loaf

1/4 cup butter
1/8 cup vegetable oil
1/4 cup sugar
1/2 cup molasses
2 tbl. brown sugar
1 tsp. baking soda
1 tsp. ginger
1 tsp. cinnamon
1/4 tsp. allspice
1 tsp. salt
3/4 cup warm milk
1 1/4 cups flour
1 tsp. baking powder
2 beaten eggs

Cream sugar, butter, and oil. Beat baking soda and molasses until fluffy. Add to sugar mixture. Add spices. Stir to blend. Add milk and eggs. Beat to blend. Add flour and baking powder. Stir to blend. Pour batter into well greased and floured loaf pan. Bake at 400 degrees for 30 minutes or until bread tests done. Cool and serve.

Body Language: Where some people have better vocabularies than others.

Glorious Morning Muffins

Makes 18 Muffins (a delicious brunch or breakfast treat)

2/3 cup raisins
2 1/2 cups flour
3/4 cup sugar
1/4 cup brown sugar
2 tsp. baking soda
2 1/4 tsp. ground cinnamon
1/2 tsp. salt
2 cups grated carrots
1 lg. tart grated apple
1/2 cup sliced almonds
1/3 cup flake coconut
4 eggs
1 cup vegetable oil
2 tsp. vanilla
1/4 tsp. lemon extract

Soak raisins in enough hot water to cover for 30 minutes. Drain well. Mix flour, sugar, baking soda, cinnamon and salt. Stir in raisins, carrots, apple, almonds and coconut. Beat eggs with oil, vanilla and extract. Blend with flour mixture lightly. Line muffin tins with paper baking cups. Divide batter into cups. Bake at 350 degrees for 20-25 minutes or until golden brown.

October 15, 1910
Dear Hannah,

Oh, how I wish I could be there to comfort you. I wept all day over your letter. I can't begin to tell you how sorry I am about Abby. What a terrible tragedy! How could something like this happen? And with Ruth and Clare only four months old! Hannah, I know those babies will be a joy to you even though the loss of your sister is still so fresh. And I'm sure their father will come back for them as soon as he gets over the shock of Abby's death. He is just grief stricken, Hannah. Give him some time to pull himself to-gether. In the meantime, shower those little girls with all the love you possibly can. You are a strong girl, Hannah. I know you can get through all this. Everything has its purpose and though all is black around you now, this pain will pass. Sur-

Hannah's Best Bran Muffins

Makes 2 1/2 dozen (forget everything you ever knew about "yucky" bran muffins. These are moist and delicious.)

3 heaping cups raisins
3 cups bran flakes
3 cups bran buds or all bran cereal
2 cups wheat germ
1 cup oatmeal
1 tsp. salt
6 cups boiling water
6 cups very hot milk
1 1/2 cups sugar
1 cup vegetable oil
4 eggs slightly beaten
3 tsp. baking soda
3 tsp. baking powder
4 -5 cups flour

Combine brans, wheat germ, oatmeal, salt, raisins, and sugar in large bowl. Add milk and water. Let stand 20 minutes or until lukewarm. Add oil and eggs. Blend well. Add flour, baking powder and baking soda (mixture should be the consistency of thick cake batter). Line muffin tins with paper baking cups. Fill cups 3/4 full. Bake at 375 degrees for 20-25 minutes or until lightly browned. Do not over bake.

Buttermilk Oatmeal Muffins

Makes 12 (terrific buttermilk flavor)

1 cup oatmeal
3/4 cup buttermilk
1/2 cup brown sugar
3/4 cup vegetable oil
1 egg (beaten)
1 cup flour
1 tsp. baking powder
1/2 tsp. baking soda
1/2 tsp. salt

round yourself with all the good memories of Abby...... remember her for those precious little girls. There will be so much they will want to know someday. Why am I so far away when you need me the most! Is there anything I can do? You will be in my prayers every day, my dear. And even though I am so far away, God is right beside you.

All my love, Emily

Buttermilk Oatmeal Muffins (cont.)

Combine oatmeal and buttermilk. Let stand 30 minutes. Combine sugar, oil, and egg into oatmeal mixture. Add remaining ingredients. Stir lightly. Line muffin tins with paper baking cups. Fill cups 2/3 full. Bake at 400 degrees until golden, about 20 minutes.

Honey Oat Muffins

Makes 12 (just TOO healthy!)

2 eggs
2/3 cup water
3 tbl. honey
2 cups oat-wheat germ
1/2 cup raisins
1/4 cup chopped nuts

Blend eggs, water, and honey. Add oat-wheat germ. Stir lightly. Fold in raisins and nuts. Line muffin tin with paper baking cups. Fill cups 2/3 full. Bake at 400 degrees for 15-20 minutes or until golden.

Huckleberry Bran Muffins

Makes 3 dozen (a berry nice change)

7 eggs
1 1/2 cups brown sugar
1/2 cup light molasses
1/4 cup honey
4 cups buttermilk
1 1/2 cups vegetable oil
1 tsp. vanilla
1/4 tsp. almond extract
2 cups bran flakes
2 cups wheat germ
1/4 cup all bran

2 cups fresh or frozen huckleberries (or blueberries)
1 1/2 cup chopped nuts (unsalted)
4 1/2 cups flour
4 tsp. baking powder
4 tsp. baking soda
1 tsp. cinnamon
1/4 tsp. nutmeg
1/4 tsp. salt

Blend eggs, sugar, molasses, and honey. Add buttermilk, oil, vanilla, and extract. Blend. Add brans and wheat germ. Blend. Let stand 20 minutes. Lightly stir in berries and nuts. Add flour, baking soda, baking powder, cinnamon, nutmeg and salt. Mix lightly. Line muffin tins with paper baking cups. Fill cups 3/4 full. Bake at 375 degrees for 20 minutes or until lightly browned.

Hard work won't kill you, but who ever heard of anybody resting to death?

Old-Fashioned Blueberry Muffins

Makes 24 (light and moist)

2 eggs
2 cups milk
1 tsp. salt
1 tsp. vanilla
2 cups vegetable oil
4 cups flour (scant)
1 cup sugar
6 tsp. baking powder
2 cups fresh or frozen (drained) blueberries

Blend eggs, milk, sugar, oil, salt and vanilla. Add flour and baking powder. Fold in blueberries. Line muffin tins with paper baking cups. Fill cups 3/4 full. Bake at 400 degrees for 20 minutes or until just golden. When cool, dust with powdered sugar, if you like!

August 10, 1913
Dear Em,

The girls are finally in bed and Andrew is still using the last available daylight to finish repairing the wagon that broke right in the middle of haying today. Aggravation seems to be his companion during harvest time.

All is well here, though over the past three years there were times when I didn't believe that life would ever be normal again. Abby's death shook me to my very foundation. It was just so unexpected. Andrew was strong for both of us...you know how he is....never says much, but he is as constant as the seasons. And how wonderful you have been. Your prayers and letters have sustained me, Emily.

Life has settled into a comfortable routine and everyone is happy. Ruth and Clare are indeed a joy. I love them as much

Apple-Cinnamon Nut Muffins

Makes 24

1 1/2 cups bran flakes
1/2 cup raisins
3/4 cup flour
1 1/4 tsp. baking soda
1/4 tsp. salt
1/2 cup buttermilk
1/2 cup vegetable oil
2 eggs
1/2 cup shredded apple
1/2 cup walnuts (chopped)
1 tbl. unsalted butter
1 1/2 tbl. sugar
1/2 tsp. cinnamon

Mix bran, raisins, flour, sugar, baking soda, and salt. Blend buttermilk and eggs. Add bran mixture and stir lightly. Let stand 20 minutes. Add remaining ingredients. Blend gently. Line muffin tins with paper baking cups. Fill 2/3 full. Bake at 400 degrees for 20-25 minutes or until lightly brown.

Emily's Self-Frosted Applesauce Muffins

Makes 18

Topping:
1/3 cup brown sugar
1/2 tsp. cinnamon

Mix together and set aside.

Muffins:
1/2 cup unsalted butter or butter flavored shortening
1 cup sugar
1 egg
2 1/2 cups flour
1 tsp. soda
1 tsp. cinnamon

as I do my own girls. As a matter of fact, I can't imagine life without them now and neither can Andrew. Poor Andrew! Life with 6 females cannot be easy, but he takes everything in stride even when all the children are so different from each other.

Ruth and Clare have absolutely nothing in common. Surprising I know, but honestly Emily, they don't even look like they could be sisters, let alone twins. In addition, their personalities are night and day. Clare is small and dark and painfully shy. She is easy to love and is always trying to please. Ruth, on the other hand, is blond and full of energy. She is into everything and is an incredible dare-devil. Yesterday, I found her in the horse corral! Be still my heart! Thank God big animals understand little children.

As for the other three, Babe is as pretty as ever,

1/2 cup raisins
1/4 cup nuts (chopped)
1 cup applesauce
1 tsp. salt
1 tsp. ground cloves

Blend butter, sugar, and egg. Add flour, soda, and spices. Stir in raisins and nuts. Mix in applesauce. Line muffin tins with paper baking cups. Fill cups 2/3 full with muffin batter. Sprinkle each cup with topping mix. Bake at 375 degrees for 25-30 minutes or until golden brown.

Cranberry-Maple Muffins

Makes 12

1 1/2 cups flour
1/4 cup almonds or walnuts
2 tsp. baking powder
1/2 tsp. salt
2 cups cranberries
1 1/4 cup sugar
2 eggs
1/2 cups unsalted butter or butter flavored shortening
1/2 cup buttermilk
2 tsp. maple flavoring

In blender process buttermilk, nuts, and cranberries on low speed until nuts and berries are thoroughly crushed but not pureed. In large bowl, blend eggs, sugar, salt, butter and maple flavoring. Add buttermilk mixture. Stir lightly. Add flour and baking powder. Stir lightly. Line muffin tins with paper baking cups. Fill cups 3/4 full. Bake at 375 degrees for 25-30 minutes or until golden.

When a man brings home flowers for no reason ..... there's a reason.

20

with an eye for expensive everything. Ranch life is definitely beneath this one. She still fights with all her sisters, but she is a good friend to me. Mary Ella is my studious one. Books and school are the center of her world.... deep thinker like her Dad. Beth thinks life inside is a bore and that she should live outside. Animals and flowers and birds and sunsets are the only things important to her. It really is funny. They are all so different, but I love them all the same. There are some things that we all like to do together. Sunday afternoons at Perry Creek picking huckleberries is certainly one of them. All of us laughing and foraging around in those bushes reminded me of you and I doing the same when we were 12. The memory gave me a moment of panic, thinking of that bear standing up right in front of us. I screamed and you

Whole Wheat Maple-Nut Muffins

Makes 12

2 tbl. sugar
2 cups whole wheat flour
1/2 cup chopped nuts
2 tsp. baking powder
2/3 cup milk
2/3 cup maple syrup
1/4 cup vegetable oil
2 eggs

Blend milk, oil, eggs, sugar, and syrup. Add flour, baking powder, and nuts. Stir lightly. Line muffin tins with paper baking cups. Fill cups 3/4 full. Bake at 400 degrees for 20 minutes or until golden brown.

Blue Ribbon Banana-Nut Muffins

Makes 18 (a real winner)

3 large ripe bananas
1 cup sugar
2 eggs
1 1/2 cups flour
1 tsp. baking powder
1 tsp. baking soda
1/2 tsp. salt
1/2 cup vegetable oil
1/2 cup chopped nuts

Mash bananas thoroughly. Blend eggs, sugar, salt, and oil. Add bananas to mixture and stir to blend. Add flour, baking soda, baking powder, and nuts. Stir lightly. Line muffin tins with paper baking cups. Fill cups 3/4 full. Bake at 375 degrees for 25 - 30 minutes or until golden brown.

took one look at that bear and didn't know whether to run or faint. The look on your face, Emily, still makes me laugh. You decided running was the better course of action, and once you started you wouldn't stop. The bear was just as scared and running faster than you in the other direction, but you were sure that he was right on your heels. I bet you are still afraid of bears. Actually, I think of you more often when I am making huckleberry peach pies than I do when I am picking berries. You really loved huckleberry pie. Remember when your Aunt Elsie was determined that you were going to learn to make pies and she tried and tried to teach you? She nearly had to drag you into the kitchen by your ankles and, in the end, you out-witted her. You paid Becky Parsons to make a pie for you and you gave it

South of the Border Corn Muffins

Makes 24 (a bit spicy, but too tasty to pass up!)

2 1/2 cups yellow cornmeal
1 cup flour
3 tsp. baking powder
1 tsp. baking soda
1 tsp. salt
12 oz. whole kernel corn
1 large grated onion
6 chopped jalapeño chilies (don't forget to seed them!)
2 cups milk
1/2 cup honey
1/2 cup vegetable oil
4 eggs

Blend eggs, honey, salt, oil, onion, chilies, and milk. Add cornmeal, flour, baking soda, and baking powder. Stir lightly. Fold in corn. Line muffin tins with paper baking cups. Fill cups 3/4 full. Bake at 400 degrees for 30 minutes or until tops split and centers are firm.

Honey Corn Muffins

Makes 18

1 1/2 cups flour
1/2 cup cornmeal
1/4 cup sugar
1 egg
1 tbl. baking powder
1 tsp. baking soda
1 tsp. salt
1/2 cup milk
1/4 cup fresh orange juice
1 tbl. lemon juice
1/4 cup butter (softened)
1/4 cup honey

to Aunt Elsie as a perfect display of your work! You imp. I wonder if Elsie ever knew.

I can see Andrew coming in from the barn and I'm sure he is tired and hungry. Will close for now. Love to Franklin and Julianna. Congratulations on your wonderful news! Hope this one will be a boy!
Love, Hannah

Blend egg, butter, sugar, and salt. Combine honey, orange juice, and lemon juice. Add to egg mixture and stir. Add flour, cornmeal, baking soda, and baking powder. Stir lightly. Add milk, stirring slowly. Do not over mix. Line muffin tins with paper baking cups. Fill cups 3/4 full. Bake at 350 degrees for 15-20 minutes or until golden.

Pumpkin Muffins

Makes 24

Topping:
2 tbl. brown sugar
1/4 tsp. cinnamon

Mix 2 tbl. brown sugar and 1/4 tsp. cinnamon together and set aside.

Muffins:
1 cup sugar
1/4 cup brown sugar
1 1/4 cups canned pumpkin
1/2 cup butter (softened)
2 eggs
1 1/2 cups flour
2 tsp. baking powder
1 tsp. cinnamon
1/4 tsp. nutmeg
1/4 tsp. salt
1 cup milk
1/2 cup chopped raisins
1/4 cup chopped nuts

Beat sugars, eggs, butter, and pumpkin until smooth. Add milk. Stir. Add flour, salt, baking powder, and spices. Stir lightly. Fold in raisins and nuts. Line muffin tins with paper baking cups. Fill cups 3/4 full. Sprinkle with topping. Bake at 400 degrees for 25 to 30 minutes or until lightly browned.

Makes 12 (rich and moist)

Freeze-Dried: When the laundry has hung on the line too long.

Topping:
1/2 cup flour
1/4 cup brown sugar
1/2 tsp. cinnamon
dash nutmeg
2 tbl. melted butter
1/4 cup chopped pecans

Combine all ingredients except pecans and stir to blend. Add nuts. Set aside.

Muffins:
6 oz. semi-sweet chocolate chips
6 oz. semi-sweet chocolate
3 tbl. butter
1 cup flour
2 tbl. sugar
2 tsp. baking powder
1/2 tsp. cinnamon
3/4 cup chopped pecans
1 egg
1/3 cup buttermilk
1/2 tsp. vanilla

Melt over low heat , 6 oz. chocolate and butter, stirring until smooth. Combine dry ingredients, chocolate chips, and pecans. Add egg, buttermilk, vanilla, and chocolate mixture. Stir to moisten. Line muffin tins with paper baking cups and fill 3/4 full with batter. Sprinkle each cup with topping. Bake at 375 degrees for 20-25 minutes or until muffins test done. Cool and serve.

Advice to wives: Do all the talking yourself. It saves time and prevents arguments.

Butterscotch-Orange Muffins

Makes 12

Topping:
6 oz. butterscotch chips
1 tbl. butter
1/2 cup flour

Melt butter and chips over low heat. Cut in flour to make crumbly mixture. Set aside.

Muffins:
1 1/2 cup flour
1/2 cup sugar
2 tbl. baking powder
1/2 tsp. salt
1/2 tsp. cinnamon
1/4 tsp. nutmeg
6 oz. butterscotch chips
1/2 cup milk
1/4 cup vegetable oil
1 egg (beaten)
1 tsp. orange rind
1/2 cup orange (finely chopped)

Combine dry ingredients. Add milk, oil, egg, orange rind, orange, and butterscotch chips. Stir to moisten. Line muffin tins with paper baking cups and fill 3/4 full with batter. Sprinkle each cup with topping. Bake at 375 degrees for 20-25 minutes or until muffins test done. Cool and serve.

25

CAKES
COOKIES
&
CANDY

CAKE TALK

There is definitely a secret to moist, delicious cakes. Cake batter likes to be thoroughly mixed making sure all ingredients are well blended. Cake pans should be greased and floured to insure easy removal after baking. When making a layer cake, freeze individual layers before frosting. Then frost frozen layers and thaw cake in refrigerator to insure a moist and perfectly frosted cake. Enjoy!

COOKIE TALK

Cookies should never be over baked...a brown cookie will most likely be dry. A golden brown color usually insures a moist, chewy cookie. Remember that cookies continue to bake for an additional minute or two after they are removed from the oven and are cooling on the pan. For the best results with drop cookies, I like to bake a test cookie to check the texture before I bake a whole pan. Cookies are always "pleasers", and they freeze well, so bake several dozen while you are at it.

CANDY TALK

Handle with care. Temperature is usually an issue with most candy recipes, and though I have used very easy recipes in this book, making candy can still be tricky at times. The effort is well worth it, though. Keep in mind that, for the most part, candy does not freeze well.

NOTES

December 24, 1915

Merry Christmas my dear Hannah!

I know you won't receive this for weeks, but I just had to say it! Everyone is asleep and I find, these days, that I do my best letter writing in the evening. Fancy that! I'm such a clever girl.

Christmas Eve has always been such a special time for me and I just wanted to share a bit of this one with you. We are having a white Christmas this year. Can you imagine.... My first white Christmas since I left Montana. Funny. Snow should be snow but somehow it isn't the same. It doesn't seem as white or as clean or as cold here in the city. It doesn't make the house look "ala mode" when you see it from a distance. And if I step outside in the evening, I can't hear the dry crackle

Buttermilk Chocolate Layer Cake

Makes one 9 inch layer cake (Unbelievable!)

2 1/2 cups flour
3/4 cup unsweetened cocoa
2 tsp. baking soda
1 tsp. salt
2 1/2 cups sugar
1 cup butter flavored shortening
2 large eggs
2 cups buttermilk
1 tsp. vanilla
1 1/2 cups chocolate pudding

Cream sugar and shortening. Add eggs and beat 2 minutes. Add flour, cocoa, baking soda, and salt. Stir to blend. Add buttermilk and vanilla. Beat 2 minutes. Pour into three well buttered and floured 9 inch round cake pans. Bake at 350 degrees for 30 minutes or until cakes test done. Cool 20 minutes. Cover cooling racks with waxed paper and invert pans onto racks. Remove cakes from pans and cool completely. Wrap in plastic wrap and freeze. While cake is freezing make Chocolate Icing. Remove from freezer and place first layer on cake platter. Spread first layer with 3/4 cup chocolate pudding. Repeat for second layer. Place third layer on top and frost. Refrigerate 12 hours before serving.

Chocolate Icing:
6 oz. unsweetened chocolate
1/2 cup butter
1 tbl. vanilla
1 1/2 cups sugar
1 cup whipping cream

Melt butter and chocolate over low heat. Add cream and sugar and stir to dissolve sugar. Remove from heat and add vanilla. Stir to blend. Chill. Whip chilled icing mixture until fluffy and light. Frost cake.

of my breath freezing the way I remember it in Montana. Nonetheless, a white Christmas is a special Christmas, and I am thankful.

This is Amanda's first Christmas, which makes it even more special. She is such fun, but what a handful. Unlike Julianna, she did not escape the Bennette strawberry hair "curse".... and she has the personality to match. I am afraid that my days of easy child rearing are over. This one is on fire! Well my dear, it looks as though neither you nor I will be the mother of a son. Seven girls between us, Hannah. It was just simply not meant to be. Franklin says that he would rather have daughters than sons anyway. Leave it to Franklin to always be the contented one.

Oh, Hannah. I was not going to tell you this in my Christmas letter.... but

Super Moist Chocolate Cake

Makes one 9 X 13 inch cake
(yummy!)

2 cups flour
1 cup unsweetened cocoa
1 1/2 tsp. baking soda
1/4 tsp. baking powder
2 cups sugar
4 eggs
1 cup mayonnaise (not salad dressing)
1/3 cup milk
1 cup water
1 cup semi-sweet chocolate chips
1 tsp. vanilla

Cream sugar, eggs, vanilla and mayonnaise. Add flour, baking soda, baking powder, and cocoa. Stir to blend. Add milk and water and beat 2 minutes. Fold in chocolate chips. Pour into well greased and floured 9 X 13 inch cake pan. Bake at 350 degrees for 30 minutes or until cake tests done. Cool. Frost with Chocolate Glaze, if desired.

Chocolate Glaze:
1/4 cup semi-sweet chocolate
1 tbl. butter
1 tsp. instant coffee

Melt chocolate and butter over low heat. Remove from heat and add instant coffee. Stir to blend. Cool slightly. Pour over cake.

A kiss is a pleasant reminder that two heads are better than one.

I must. My life is over! Leona is coming to live with us! I was thunder-struck when Franklin offered. I felt like my legs would not hold me up long enough to get me into a chair. Well, you know, she has never married. She is nearly 50 years of age and not in good health. She just can't live alone any more. But why here? I am beside myself. She has never liked me and has made it her business to mind mine ever since I met her. I can never do anything right in her eyes. How will I ever manage? Julianna loves her, but then, Julianna loves everybody. Amanda doesn't like her, but then, Amanda doesn't like anybody. Franklin...well you know Franklin...the soft heart. As for me, I'm nothing but jelly when I'm around her. It looks like I'm really stuck this time. It's your turn to pray, Hannah.

Have a very Merry

Chocolate-Zucchini Cake

Makes one 9 X 13 inch cake

1 1/3 cups sugar
1/2 cup butter
1/2 cup vegetable oil
1/2 cup milk
1 tsp. orange juice
2 eggs
1 tsp. vanilla
1/2 tsp. almond extract
2 1/2 cups flour
1/2 cup unsweetened cocoa
1 tsp. baking soda
1/2 tsp. allspice
1 tsp. cinnamon
1/2 tsp. baking powder
pinch of salt
2 cups grated zucchini
powdered sugar

Beat sugar, butter, and oil together until light. Add milk and orange juice. Stir to blend. Add eggs, vanilla, and almond extract. Beat 1 minute. Add flour, cocoa, baking powder, baking soda, spices and salt. Stir to blend. Fold in zucchini. Pour into 9 X 13 inch well greased and floured cake pan. Bake at 325 degrees for 40 minutes or until cake tests done. Cool. Sprinkle with powdered sugar. Cut and serve.

Three rules for healthy teeth: Brush after every meal, see your dentist twice a year, and mind your own business.

Chocolate Applesauce Cupcakes

Makes 24

3/4 cup butter flavored shortening
1 1/2 cups sugar
2 eggs
3 tsp. water
2 cups applesauce
2 cups flour
1 cup unsweetened cocoa
2 tsp. baking soda
2 tsp. cinnamon
1/2 tsp. allspice
dash of nutmeg
1/2 cup walnuts (finely chopped)

Cream shortening and sugar. Add eggs and beat 1 minute. Add water and applesauce and stir to blend. Add dry ingredients and beat 2 minutes. Line muffin tins with paper baking cups and fill cups 2/3 full with batter. Bake at 350 degrees for 20 minutes or until cup cakes spring back when touched. Cool 5 minutes. Remove from muffin tins and cool on racks. Frost with Chocolate Icing.

Chocolate-Chip Cheese Cupcakes

Makes 24 (so moist..no need for frosting!)

3 cups flour
2 cups sugar
1/2 cup unsweetened cocoa
1 egg
1 tsp salt
2 tsp. baking soda
2/3 cup vegetable oil
2 cups water
2 tbl. vinegar
2 tbl. vanilla

Combine flour, sugar, cocoa, salt, and baking soda. Add oil, egg, water, vinegar and vanilla. Beat 1 minute. Line muffin tins with paper baking cups and fill 2/3 full with batter. Set aside.

Filling:
16 oz. cream cheese (softened)
1 egg
1/3 cup sugar
1/4 tsp. salt
12 oz semi-sweet chocolate chips

Whip first 4 ingredients until pale and light. Fold in chocolate chips. Drop heaping teaspoons of mixture into batter filled cups, dividing mixture evenly into all cups. Bake at 350 degrees for 20 minutes or until cupcakes test done. Cool 5 minutes. Remove from muffin tins and cool on racks.

Apple-Nut Coffee Cake

Makes one 8 inch square cake

3 cups shredded tart apples
1 cup chopped walnuts
1/2 cup shredded coconut
1/2 cup raisins
1 1/2 cups flour
1 tsp. baking powder
1 tsp. cinnamon
1 tsp. allspice
2 eggs
3/4 cup brown sugar
1/2 cup white sugar
1 tsp. vanilla
3/4 cup sour cream

Combine first 8 ingredients. Beat remaining ingredients together until light and fluffy. Fold in dry ingredients. Stir to blend. Pour into well greased 8 inch square baking pan.

Age is a high price to pay for maturity.

Apple-Nut Coffee Cake (cont.)

Bake at 350 degrees for 45 minutes or until cake tests done. Cool. Cut into squares. Top with whipped cream. Serve.

Don't treat your body like you had a spare in the trunk.

Oatmeal Caramel Coffee Cake

Makes one 9 X 13 inch cake

1 cup oatmeal
1 1/4 cups boiling water
2 eggs
1 cup sugar
1 cup brown sugar
1/2 cup vegetable oil
1 1/2 cups flour
1 tsp. baking soda
1 tsp. salt
1 tsp. cinnamon

Combine oatmeal and water and set aside. Beat eggs, sugars and oil. Add flour, baking soda, salt, and cinnamon. Stir to blend. Stir in oatmeal mixture. Pour into well greased and floured 9 X 13 inch cake pan. Bake at 350 degrees for 30 minutes or until cake tests done. Sprinkle topping over warm cake.

Topping:
1 cup shredded coconut
1 cup brown sugar
6 tbl. melted butter
1/2 cup chopped pecans
1/4 cup evaporated milk

Combine all ingredients just to moisten. Sprinkle over cake.

The best way to remember your wife's birthday is to forget it once!

April 22, 1919
Dear Emily,

I was sitting looking out the window one morning last month, watching what I thought was surely the last snow fall of the winter. The children were all in school, Andrew had gone over to Billy Johnston's to look at a bull and I had just poured myself a cup of tea. I was lost in some sort of silly daydream when I saw something moving out of the corner of my eye. I got up and went to the kitchen door. I opened it and stepped outside (wearing nothing but my house dress mind you). I didn't see anything so I leaned around the corner of the house to get a better look. Emily, have you ever seen a moose close up? I mean really close up? They are big.....very big. Take my word for it. This particular moose was not more than 18 inches from

Farm Cream Coffee Cake

Makes one 9 X 13 inch cake

Topping:
1 cup brown sugar
5 tbl. chopped nuts
2 tbl. cinnamon
1/4 cup shredded coconut

Combine all ingredients and set aside.

3 cups flour
2 tsp. baking soda
1/4 tsp. salt
1 cup butter (softened)
2 cups sugar
4 eggs
2 cups coddled cream or sour cream
2 tsp. vanilla

Cream butter and sugar until fluffy. Add eggs and beat. Add sour cream and vanilla and stir to blend. Add dry ingredients. Stir. Pour batter into well greased 9 X 13 inch baking pan. Sprinkle with topping mixture. Bake at 350 degrees 45 minutes or until cake tests done. Cool. Serve.

Old-fashioned Raisin Spice Cake

Makes one 9 inch layer cake

3 cups flour
2 cups sugar
1 cup mayonnaise (not salad dressing)
1/3 cup milk
2 eggs
2 tsp. baking soda
1 tsp. cinnamon
1 tsp. allspice
dash nutmeg
3 cups shredded tart apples
1 cup raisins
1/2 cup chopped nuts

my face. I was so scared
that I couldn't even
scream, which of course,
meant that I couldn't move
either. So, like a dummy,
I just stood there shivering
(or trembling I'm not sure
which). Her eyes were like
two huge lumps of coal and
they got wider as she
breathed harder. She took
a step forward. I took one
backward. The scene
repeated itself. And then
she came right up on the
porch after me. Well, let
me tell you, I was beyond
"mad scramble" long before
I got to the kitchen door
and hysterical by the time I
was behind it. The moose
was just plain mad.
Imagine the nerve of that
beast to smash the glass in
my brand new kitchen door!
Well, then I got mad. I
snatched Andrew's rifle
from behind the wood box,
closed my eyes and fired.
The look on Andrew's
face! A semi-demolished
kitchen door and a com-

Old-fashioned Raisin Spice Cake (cont.)

Combine all ingredients except fruit and nuts. Blend well. Add fruit and nuts. Stir to blend (mixture will be very thick). Pour into well greased and floured 9 inch cake pans. Bake at 350 degrees for 45 minutes or until cake tests done. Cool 5 minutes and turn out of pans. Cool. Wrap individual cakes in plastic wrap and freeze. Remove plastic wrap and place first layer on cake platter. Spread with frosting. Position second layer and frost entire cake. (Frost with Vanilla Fluff Frosting.) Defrost cake in refrigerator. Sprinkle with cinnamon. Serve.

Vanilla Fluff Frosting:
5 tbl. flour
1 cup sugar
1 cup butter
1 tsp. vanilla
1 cup milk
Combine milk and flour in tightly covered jar and shake to blend. Pour into sauce pan and cook over low heat until thickened. Cool. Chill. Cream butter, sugar, and vanilla. Gradually add chilled flour mixture, beating at high speed until light and fluffy. Frost.

White Cloud Coconut Cake

Makes one 8 inch layer cake

2 1/3 cup coconut
2 cups flour
1 tbl. baking powder
1/4 tsp. salt
3 egg whites
2 tsp. white vinegar
1 3/4 cups sugar
1/2 cup butter
1 tsp. rum extract
1 tsp. vanilla extract
1/2 tsp. almond extract
3/4 cup milk

pletely dead moose. Not exactly two birds with one stone. The children are having great fun with this story and Frank Miller called me "Annie Oakley" when I was in the feed store last week. Cheeky bugger.

Anyway, this whole thing is truly funny now. Reminded me of Bud and Phylis Baker and their "bear on the porch" story. You remember, Em. Same sort of thing, except Bud ended up on the porch with a .22 rifle. Phylis panicked and shut the door when the bear charged. Poor Bud was running backwards and trying to shoot the intruder at the same time. All the racket he made falling over the chair and then through the railing of the porch scared the bear off, I guess. He was lying on the ground, stuck in the broken railing, as I recall. He was so mad at Phylis for laughing at him that he swore he

Whip whites and gradually add vinegar and continue until whites are firm. Cream butter and sugar until fluffy. Add extracts and milk. Beat 1 minute. Add flour, baking powder and salt. Stir to blend. Fold in 2 cups coconut. Pour into well greased and floured 8 inch cake pans. Bake at 350 degrees for 25 minutes or until cake tests done. Cool completely and frost with marshmallow frosting. Sprinkle with remaining coconut.

No-cook Marshmallow Frosting:
1/4 tsp. salt
2 egg whites
1/4 cup sugar
3/4 cup light corn syrup
1 1/2 tsp. vanilla

Add salt to egg whites and beat to soft peak. Gradually add sugar and beat until glossy. Slowly add syrup, beating until thoroughly firm peaks form. Fold in vanilla. Use frosting immediately.

Whole Wheat Honey-Pineapple Cake

Makes one 9 X 13 inch cake

2 eggs (beaten)
1/2 cup honey
2 cups whole wheat flour
1/2 tsp salt
2 tsp. baking soda
3/4 cup chopped nuts
2 1/2 cups crushed pineapple (with juice)
1 cup diced dates
1/2 cup shredded coconut
1/2 cup dry milk

was going to feed her to the next bear he saw.

Well, I would not have believed it if I hadn't heard it straight from Doc Torgeson's own lips yesterday. I'm pregnant again. Or am I expecting? I can never remember which. Wouldn't you just know it. They say "never give your baby clothes and diapers away, because you will surely get pregnant". I did and I am. Andrew is praying for a boy and so are the girls. I just want it to be healthy, but if it is a boy, I'll be thrilled. This one should be born around the first of September. Six children, Emily! People will think we have no self control what-so-ever! Andrew said he knew a month ago. He says my cheeks get pink. How embarrassing.

My love to all,
Hannah

Whole Wheat Honey-Pineapple Cake (cont.)

Mix eggs and honey. Add flour, baking soda, nuts, and salt. Stir to blend. Add pineapple, dates, coconut and dry milk. Stir to blend. Pour batter into well greased 9 X 13 inch cake pan. Bake at 350 degrees for 35 minutes or until cake tests done. Cool. Sprinkle with powdered sugar.

Lemon Almond Pound Cake

Makes one loaf cake

3 cups flour
1/2 tsp. baking powder
1/4 tsp. salt
1 cup butter (softened)
1/2 cup shortening
3 cups sugar
5 eggs
1/2 cup lemon juice
1/2 cup milk
1 tsp. almond extract

Combine lemon juice and milk. Cream shortening, butter, and sugar. Add eggs and beat 1 minute. Add flour, baking powder, and salt. Stir to blend. Add lemon juice mixture and extract. Beat to blend. Pour into well greased and floured loaf pan. Bake at 350 degrees for 1 hour and 15 minutes or until cake tests done. Cool 5 minutes. Turn out of pan. Cool completely and dust with powdered sugar.

May your life be like a roll of toilet paper .... long and useful.

Summer Fresh Strawberry Shortcake

Serves 6

3 pints fresh strawberries (sliced)
1/4 cup honey
4 tsp. lemon juice
2 cups flour
2 tbl. sugar
3 tsp. baking powder
1/2 tsp. salt
1/4 cup shortening
1/4 cup sour cream
3 tbl. softened butter
milk
whipping cream

Combine strawberries, honey, and lemon juice. Let stand 1 hour. Combine dry ingredients. Cut in shortening and butter. Lightly mix in sour cream and add just enough milk to make soft dough. Roll out on floured board. Cut into 3 inch diameter biscuits and bake on lightly greased cookie sheet at 400 degrees for 20 minutes or until golden. While still hot split in half. Top with strawberries and whipped cream. Serve.

Emily's Holiday Fruit Cake

Makes one bundt cake (not your usual fruit cake!)

6 egg whites
3 cups flour
1/4 tsp. baking soda
1/8 tsp. salt
2 cups sugar
1 cup softened butter
6 egg yolks
1 cup sour cream
1 tsp. vanilla

February 3, 1920
Dear Hannah,

Finally a boy! I can just imagine Andrew. Will you ever be able to wipe the grin off his face? Andrew David Hansen, Jr. What an impressive name. Oh, please don't call him A.J., Hannah. I know how you love nicknames, but a handsome little lad shouldn't have to answer to a name with no vowels. A.J. sounds like a gangster or someones pet, for heaven's sake. Your beautiful Augusta called "Babe", of all things. And then you took a wonderful name like Elizabeth Ann Marie and shortened it to "Beth". And now A.J.? If you ever have another one, you probably won't bother to name it at all.

What wonderful news about Augusta. (Thank goodness she had enough sense to call herself by her given name.) It is inconceivable that she is en-

1 tsp. almond extract
1/2 cup chopped walnuts
1/2 cup chopped pecans
12 oz. mixed candied fruit

Mix dry ingredients together. Beat whites until soft peak. Gradually add 1 cup sugar and beat until stiff. Cream butter and remaining sugar. Add yolks and beat 1 minute. Add extracts and dry ingredients. Stir to blend. Fold in whites, nuts and fruit. Pour batter into well greased and powdered sugar dusted bundt pan. Bake at 350 degrees 1 hour or until cake is firm but not dry. Cool completely. Store in airtight container. Refrigerate.

Bittersweet Brownies

Makes 3 doz. (just sweet enough)

Brownies:
1 1/2 cups flour
1 cup unsweetened cocoa
1 1/2 tsp. salt
1 1/4 tsp. baking powder
1 cup butter flavored shortening
2 cups sugar
3 eggs
1/4 cup light corn syrup
2 tsp. vanilla
1 cup chopped walnuts (optional)

Cream shortening, sugar, and salt together. Add eggs and blend. Add syrup and vanilla. Mix. Add dry ingredients. Mix well. Stir in nuts (optional). Grease 9 X 13 inch baking pan. Spread mixture into pan evenly. Bake at 350 degrees until edges are slightly firm but center is still soft. Cool and frost.

gaged. He's not really moving her to San Francisco when they are married this summer? I know you will miss her, Hannah. But I suppose being an accountant means that he needs to live in a big city. How I would love to come to the wedding, but you and I both know that with all my responsibilities here, it is simply not possible.

Franklin's business is growing by leaps and bounds. He is working much too hard and I worry about his health. He seems happier than I have ever seen him, though. Perhaps some people thrive on hard work and busy schedules. I am definitely not one of them. I know I should take the word "yes" out of my vocabulary, and I do say no, but nobody listens. Now don't start, Hannah. You have admonished me more than once on this very issue. Old habits are hard to break. This year, I am on the board of The Ladies

Chocolate Icing:
2 tbl. butter
1 tsp. shortening
3 oz. unsweetened chocolate
2 tsp. vanilla
2 cups powdered sugar

Melt butter and shortening over low heat. Blend in vanilla. Remove from heat and stir in powdered sugar. (Thin with warm water if needed.) Spread over cooled brownies. Let stand 20 minutes to set icing. Cut into 2 inch squares. Devour.

Triple Layer Fudge Brownies

Makes 2 doz. (a texture adventure)

Layer One:
1/2 cup flour
1/4 tsp. baking soda
1/4 tsp. salt
1 cup quick oats
1/2 cup brown sugar
6 tbl. melted butter

Combine flour, soda, salt, oatmeal, and brown sugar. Add butter and stir to blend. Pat mixture into bottom of 11 X 7 inch greased baking pan. Bake at 350 degrees for 10 to 15 minutes or until lightly brown.

Layer Two:
3/4 cups sugar
1/4 cup butter
2 oz. unsweetened chocolate
1 egg

Melt sugar, butter, and chocolate together over low heat. Cool. Beat egg and add to mixture. Set aside.

1 cup flour
1/3 tsp. baking powder

Aid Society and 3 charities. In addition, I am chairwoman of the Church Social Committee. I take Amanda with me as often as possible, and though she is a constant source of public embarrassment, I find her antics quite humorous. What a character she is! She reminds me of you, Hannah. As a matter of fact, her aggressive nature and her annoying habit of "speaking her mind" are exactly like you. I thank God daily that you are not here to influence her.

In your last letter, you asked about Leona. She still infuriates me daily. For a while I thought she would drive me mad. I felt like a prisoner in my own home, but then something happened that has changed my view of Leona considerably. I was in the kitchen drying dishes and muttering under my breath about something nasty Leona had said to me.

1/4 tsp. salt
1/2 cup chopped nuts
1/3 cup vegetable oil
1/2 cup sour cream
1/2 tsp. vanilla

Combine flour, baking powder, salt, and nuts. Gradually add chocolate mixture and oil. Stir to blend. Add sour cream and vanilla. Mix well. Pour over layer one and bake at 350 degrees for 20 minutes, or until firm. Do not over bake.

Layer Three:
1 oz. unsweetened chocolate
2 tbl. butter
1 1/2 cup powdered sugar
1 tsp. vanilla
warm water

Melt chocolate and butter over low heat. Remove from heat and add vanilla. Add powdered sugar and beat until smooth. Thin with warm water until mixture is consistancy of heavy syrup. Smooth over warm brownies and let stand 20 minutes to set. Cut into 2 inch squares.

Peanut Butter-Caramel Brownies

Makes 3 doz.

Filling:
1 1/4 cup extra chunky peanut butter
3/4 cup caramel ice cream topping
1 egg yolk

Stir all ingredients together until well blended and refrigerate.

Brownies:
1/2 cup butter flavored shortening

Julianna was sitting quietly on the window seat listening to my fuming. I suppose I stopped long enough to take a breath and Julianna gently seized the opportunity to say something she must have been trying to say to me for months. She said. "Mamma, Auntie Lee doesn't have any friends. She is so unhappy and she doesn't feel good most of the time. Couldn't you be her friend?" Out of the mouths of babes. She was right, of course. I have always tried to avoid Leona rather than include her. How awful this must have made her feel. I put down the dish towel and took a brisk walk up the stairs to Leona's room. Hannah, I didn't even knock. I just walked in. (Very inappropriate, I know, but I had a purpose, you see.) Leona was sitting by the window in that blue velvet chair that she always favors. She

Peanut Butter-Caramel Brownies (cont.)

4 oz. unsweetened chocolate
1 cup flour
1/2 tsp. baking powder
1/4 tsp. salt
1 cup brown sugar
1/2 cup sugar
4 large eggs

Melt shortening and chocolate over low heat. Cool. Beat eggs, sugars, and salt together. Gradually add chocolate mixture. Stir to blend. Add remaining ingredients. Mix well. Pour 1/2 of mixture into well greased 9 X 13 inch baking pan. Place in freezer for 15 minutes. Drop filling mixture in small balls onto brownie batter at even intervals (6 rows of 6). Pour remaining brownie batter evenly over the top. Cover tightly with foil and bake at 325 degrees for 30 minutes. Remove foil and continue to bake for an additional 35 minutes or until brownies are firm but not dry.

Black & Gold Brownies

Makes 2 doz.

2 1/2 cups graham cracker crumbs
2 cups sweetened condensed milk (not evaporated milk)
6 oz. semi-sweet chocolate chips
1/2 cup chopped nuts

Combine all ingredients together and mix well. Pour into well greased 8 inch square baking pan. Bake at 350 degrees for 30 minutes or until golden. Cool 10 minutes and cut into squares.

If you have half a mind to get married...do it. That's all it takes!

turned and glared at me with that cold stare that normally wilts me. I took a deep breath and gathered my courage. "Leona", I said. " Would you like to go with me to the church bazzar on Friday? I think it would be great fun, and afterwards perhaps we could go to The Cranston for lunch." I was not prepared for the tears either of us shed that morning. It was as though years of aggravation and heartache melted away. Make no mistake. We still have our tense moments, Leona and I. But life is easier. The real change being that we tend to argue to finish the problem, rather than fuming privately. Thank God for the love and faith of children.

I will close for now. Franklin is coming up the walk. How do I know? I

Montana Oatmeal Brownies

Makes 4 doz.

3/4 cup melted butter
1 cup brown sugar
1/4 cup sugar
6 cups quick oats
1/2 cup flour
2 tsp. baking soda
2 tsp. cinnamon
2 eggs slightly beaten

Combine all ingredients together. Press mixture firmly and evenly into 9 X 13 inch baking pan. Bake at 350 degrees for 15 minutes. Reduce temperature to 300 degrees and continue baking for 25 minutes. Cool completely. Cut into squares.

Babe Ruth Bars

Makes 2 doz.

Bars:
1 cup sugar
1 cup brown sugar
1 1/2 cup light corn syrup
1 cup crunchy peanut butter
7 cups corn flakes
1 cup peanuts

Cook sugar and syrup over low heat, stirring constantly. Boil 1 minute. Stir in peanut butter. Melt together. Add corn flakes and peanuts. Stir lightly to mix. Pour into 9 X 13 inch well greased baking pan and smooth to fill pan evenly.

Topping:
12 oz. semi-sweet chocolate
2 tbl. butter
3 tbl. creamy peanut butter

Melt together over low heat and pour over bar mixture. Cool. Cut into 1 X 2 inch bars.

Rocky Road Bars

Makes 1 doz.

1/2 cup butter flavored shortening
1/2 cup brown sugar
1 tsp. vanilla
1 tsp. cinnamon
1 cup flour
1/2 cup graham cracker crumbs
6 oz. chocolate chips
1 cup tiny marshmallows
1/2 cup chopped walnuts

Cream shortening, sugar, vanilla, and cinnamon until creamy. Add flour and graham crackers. Mix well. Pat into well greased 8 X 8 inch baking pan. Cover with chocolate chips, marshmallows, and nuts. Bake at 275 degrees for 20 minutes or until marshmallows are melted and golden. Cool and cut into 1 inch squares.

Turtle Bars

Makes 2 doz.

1/4 cup butter (melted)
1 cup graham cracker crumbs
1 cup semi-sweet chocolate chips
1 cup coconut (shredded)
1 cup chopped pecans
1/3 cup sweetened condensed milk

Combine butter and graham cracker crumbs. Stir in condensed milk to moisten and pour into 9 X 13 inch baking pan. Press evenly into bottom of pan. Combine chocolate chips, nuts, and coconut. Sprinkle mixture over graham crackers. Bake at 350 degrees for 25 minutes.

A minor operation is one performed on someone else.

My husband and I have a magical relationship. I ask him to do the dishes and he disappears.

Chewy Raisin-Oatmeal Bars

Makes 2 doz.

1 cup butter
2/3 cup powdered sugar
1 1/8 cups flour
1 1/2 cups flaked coconut
1 1/4 cups quick oats
3 eggs
1 tsp. vanilla
1 cup brown sugar
1/4 cup honey
1 tsp. baking powder
1 cup raisins

Whip butter until fluffy. Gradually beat in powdered sugar and honey. Stir in 1 cup flour, 1/2 cup coconut, and quick oats. Press into ungreased 9 inch square baking pan. Bake at 350 degrees for 20 minutes or until golden brown. Beat eggs, vanilla, and brown sugar. Stir in remaining flour and baking powder. Stir in raisins and remaining coconut. Pour over pre-baked crust and bake 30 minutes. Cool. Dust with powdered sugar. Cut into 2 inch squares.

Date Bars

Makes 1 doz.

3/4 cup flour
1 tsp. baking powder
1/4 tsp. salt
3 egg yolks
3 egg whites
1 cup sugar
1 cup chopped nuts
3/4 pound pitted dates (diced)

Beat yolks until pale. Gradually beat in sugar. Stir in nuts and dates. Stir in dry ingredients. Using clean utensils, beat egg whites until stiff and fold into mixture. Bake at 350 degrees in 8 inch square baking pan for 20 minutes or until golden. Cool and cut into bars.

Honey-Nut Granola Bars

Makes 2 doz.

1 3/4 cups butter
1/3 cup brown sugar
1/3 cup honey
1 tsp. vanilla
1/2 tsp. salt
4 cups granola
1/3 cup chopped walnuts
1/3 cup sesame seeds
1/2 cup flaked coconut

Combine butter, sugar, and honey and blend well. Add vanilla and salt. Beat until smooth. Stir in granola, seeds and nuts. Mix thoroughly. Press evenly into well greased 10 X 15 inch pan. Bake 15 minutes or until golden. Cool and cut into bars.

"Easy as Pie" Cherry Squares

Makes 1 doz.

1 cup butter (softened)
2 cups sugar
4 eggs
1 tsp. cinnamon
1 1/2 tsp. vanilla
1 tsp. almond extract
3 cups flour
1 (21 oz.) can cherry pie filling

Cream sugar and butter. Beat in eggs. Add vanilla, cinnamon, and almond extract. Blend in flour. Pour half of batter into a 9 X 13 greased glass baking pan. Top with cherry filling. Pour remaining batter over. Bake at 350 degrees until golden and firm to touch (about 30 minutes). Cool. Cut and serve.

You know it is time to diet when you nod one chin and the others second the motion.

September 10, 1924
Dear Emily,

Impossible! A.J. celebrated his 5th birthday last week and Patrick his 1st just the month before. Mary Ella is off to college and Augusta is "expecting" a baby in November. She says that the baby is due on my birthday! Insult to injury. A baby of my own, still in diapers, and I'm about to become a grandmother on my 38th birthday! I will have to spend the rest of my life with a paper bag over my head. Andrew finds the whole thing quite hilarious and teases me unmercifully. I remind him, however, that he is the father of that one year old and he too, is about to become a grandparent. Doesn't bother him a bit, but then nothing ever does. He is just an old farmer....and I love him for it!

Mary Ella is attending a teachers college in Illinois. She left two

Blueberries 'n Cheese Squares

Makes 1 doz.

1 1/2 cups graham cracker crumbs
1/2 cup powdered sugar
2/3 cup butter (melted)
1/2 cup sugar
1/2 cup brown sugar
8 oz. cream cheese (softened)
2 eggs (beaten)
2 1/2 tbl. lemon juice
1 (21 oz.) can blueberry pie filling
dash nutmeg

Mix crumbs, powdered sugar, and butter. Press into 9 X 13 inch baking pan. Mix sugars, eggs, cream cheese, and nutmeg until smooth. Spread over crust. Bake 20 minutes at 350 degrees. Cool. Stir lemon juice into pie filling. Spread over top of baked cheese mixture. Chill. Serve. Top with whipped cream.

Luscious Lemon Squares

Makes 1 doz.

Cookie Crust:
1 cup butter (melted)
dash salt
1/2 cup sugar
2 cups flour

Combine all ingredients and press into greased 9 X 13 inch baking pan. Bake 15 minutes at 350 degrees until golden. Cool.

Lemon Filling:
2 cups sugar
1/4 cup flour
4 beaten eggs
6 tbl. lemon juice

weeks ago and I miss my "little book worm" miserably. She is the only person on either side of our family tree that has ever been to college! All eyes will be on her. She will do fine. She was always a good student and I'm sure she will be an excellent teacher.

Clare has become my "home body". I love her so much, and what a helper she is. You would think that baby Patrick (we call him "Mr. no name" just for fun sometimes) is her baby instead of her baby brother. She does worry me a bit though, Em. She still is so painfully shy. A sharp word or teasing can just crush her and she cries at the drop of the hat. In retrospect, 14 was a hard age for me, too, so maybe she will grow out of it.

Ruth is still Ruth. I would be willing to bet that your Amanda and my Ruth are quite a bit alike. Ruth is probably more of a tomboy, I expect. This

Combine sugar and flour. Mix in beaten eggs. Add lemon juice and stir. Pour over crust. Bake at 350 degrees or until firm but not dry. Cool completely and sprinkle with powdered sugar. Cut into 2 inch squares. Serve.

Hannah's Best Chocolate Chip Cookie

Makes 3 doz. (big & chewy)

1 1/2 cups shortening
1 1/2 cups butter flavored shortening
2 cups sugar
2 cups brown sugar
2 tsp. salt
1 tbl. vanilla
4 eggs
2 tsp. baking soda
6-7 cups flour
2 (12 oz.) packages semi-sweet chocolate chips
1/2 cup chopped walnuts (optional)

Pre-heat oven to 350 degrees. Bake cookies about 10 minutes or until golden but not brown. Do not over bake.

Mix shortenings, sugars, vanilla, and salt. Add eggs and beat 1 minute. Add baking soda and gradually add 6 cups flour until mixture is thick but not dry. Bake a small test cookie. Cookie should be well formed, moist and chewy. If cookie is thin, flat, and crunchy at edges, add more flour.

When test cookie bakes perfect, add chocolate chips and nuts. Stir to mix. Drop tablespoon sized cookies onto ungreased cookie sheet about 2 inches apart (usually 12 cookies to a sheet). Do not flatten dough. Bake. Cool 3 minutes on sheet and remove to cool completely on waxed paper.

summer she brought home a ferret. Andrew was concerned, Clare was aghast, and I found the idea completely distasteful, to say the very least. When you live in the country you expect to have animals in and out of your house.... but a ferret? This was too much for me. I insisted that the rodent had to be in a cage if it was to live in my house. I explained to Ruth that I would never be able to sleep with an animal roaming loose. To make a long story very short, the blasted bugger escaped and ended up as an unexpected bedfellow with Andrew and me. Chaos ensued. We must have scared the darn thing half to death because we haven't seen it since. I don't sleep easy, though. I'm waiting for "Act Two".

Beth has become her fathers right hand. She has always preferred to be outdoors. I argued with

Mexican Wedding Cake Cookies

Makes 2 doz. (delicate and light)

1 cup butter
1 tsp. vanilla
3/4 cup powdered sugar
1 cup chopped nuts
1 3/4 cups flour
1 tbl. dry instant coffee

Mix all ingredients together and form into small bite-sized balls. Bake on ungreased cookie sheet at 250 degrees for 30 minutes. Do not brown. When cookies are warm (not hot), roll in powdered sugar. Serve.

Cream Cheese Cookies

Makes 2 doz. (melt in your mouth)

1 cup shortening
3 oz. cream cheese (softened)
1 cup sugar
1 egg
1 tsp. vanilla
2 1/4 cups flour
1/2 tsp. salt
1/4 tsp. baking powder

Blend shortening, cream cheese, and sugar. Add egg and vanilla. Beat one minute. Add flour, salt, and baking powder. Mix well. Chill 1/2 hour. Drop teaspoon-sized cookies onto ungreased cookie sheet 2 inches apart. Bake at 350 degrees for 8-10 minutes or until golden but not brown. Cool. Frost with your favorite icing or dust with powdered sugar. Serve.

Martyr: Someone who suffers in silence louder than anyone you know!

her for years over cooking, sewing, and housekeeping, but finally gave up. If she wants to be a rancher, let her be a rancher. After all, to each her own. I think.

A.J. is definitely his fathers son....cut off the same limb, those too. The two of them are off together hunting or fishing whenever Andrew has a chance. The first time the two of them went fishing, Andrew was such a proud papa. He was taking his son out to teach him to fish. Well guess who caught all the fish? And guess who didn't even get a nibble? Emily. I thought I would die laughing as I eavesdropped from the kitchen window. They were cleaning A.J.'s fish on the back porch and A.J. said to his dad, "Thanks for taking me fishing, Dad. It's really easy, isn't it?"

And Patrick.....what can I say. He is the happiest, most contented

Spiced Apple Cookie

Makes 1 (Enormous! You'll love it)

1 1/2 cups chopped dried apples
1/2 cup raisins
1/3 cup frozen apple juice concentrate (thawed)
1/4 cup honey
1 tbl. lemon juice
1 1/2 cups flour
1/2 cup sugar
1/2 tsp. salt
1/2 tsp. cinnamon
1/2 tsp. allspice
1/3 cup butter flavored shortening
1 lg. egg
2 tsp. vanilla
1 cup chopped nuts

Combine apples, juices, honey, and raisins and simmer over low heat for 15 minutes. Cover and cool. Add lemon juice and stir. Blend dry ingredients together. Cut in shortening. Stir in egg and vanilla. Add apple mixture and stir. Add nuts. Foil line one 12 inch pizza pan making sure foil folds over edges. Grease and flour foil. Press mixture into pan evenly. Bake at 350 degrees for 30 minutes or until golden brown. Let cool 5 minutes. Slide cookie (foil and all) out of pan onto cooling rack and cool completely. Frost.

Icing:
6 tbl. powdered sugar
1 1/2 tbl. whipping cream
1 tsp. almond extract

Blend together until smooth. Frost cookie and cut into wedges. Serve.

A vacation is what you take when you can no longer take what you have been taking.

baby I have ever seen.
Handsome lad...looks just
like me.

Goodbye for now, dear
Emily. I have bread in
the oven and dozens of
things left to do before
dinner.

Love to all, Hannah

Toasted Maple-Pecan Cookies

Makes 3 doz. (yummy!)

1 1/2 cups butter flavored shortening
1/2 cup powdered sugar
1/2 cup sugar
1 tsp. vanilla
1 tsp. maple flavoring
1/2 tsp. salt
2 cups finely chopped pecans

Cream butter, sugars, and flavorings. Add remaining ingredients. Stir to blend. Add nuts. Chill 1 hour. Drop teaspoon sized cookies onto ungreased cookie sheet about 2 inches apart. Bake at 350 degrees until golden but not brown. Cool. Serve.

Danish Butter Cookies

Makes 3 doz. (lightly flavored and chewy)

2 cups butter flavored shortening
3 cups powdered sugar
3 eggs
2 tsp. vanilla
2 tsp. cream of tartar
1/4 tsp. ground cardamon
2 tsp. baking soda
5 cups flour
1/2 tsp. salt

Blend shortening, sugar, vanilla, salt, eggs, and cardamon. Add cream of tartar, soda and flour. Mix thoroughly. Drop teaspoon-sized cookies onto ungreased baking sheet about 2 inches apart. Dip bottom of drinking glass in sugar and flatten each cookie slightly. Bake at 350 degrees for about 8 minutes or until just barely golden. Do not over bake. Cool and serve.

When we were twenty we planned for what we would do at forty, but when we are sixty we plan for what we will do after breakfast.

Peanut Butter Crunch Cookies

Makes 3 doz. (this is a serious cookie!)

2 cups sugar
1 cup brown sugar
1 cup butter flavored shortening
1 cup crunchy peanut butter
1/2 cup water
2 tsp. vanilla
2 eggs
6 cups oatmeal
2 cups flour
1/2 tsp. salt
1 tsp. baking soda
1 cup raisins

Mix sugars, shortening, eggs, vanilla, salt, peanut butter, and water. Beat 1 minute. Add oatmeal, soda, flour, and raisins. Drop teaspoon-sized cookies onto ungreased cookie sheet about 2 inches apart. Bake at 350 degrees for 8-10 minutes. Cool.

Best Date Cookie

Makes 6 doz.

1 lb. pitted whole dates
3 oz. walnut or pecan halves
(actually, same number of nuts and dates)
1 tsp. vanilla
1/4 cup butter
3/4 cup brown sugar
1 egg
1 1/4 cups flour
1/2 tsp. baking soda
1/2 tsp. salt
1/2 cup sour cream

When a girl drinks like a fish almost any old line will land her.

Best Date Cookie (cont.)

Stuff dates with nut halves. Cream butter, sugar, and vanilla. Beat in egg. Add dry ingredients alternately with sour cream. Stir to blend well. Gently stir in dates. Drop tablespoon-sized cookies onto ungreased baking sheet USING ONE DATE PER COOKIE. Bake at 400 degrees for 8-10 minutes. Cool. Roll in powdered sugar or frost.

Macaroon Madness

Makes 3 doz.

2 1/2 cups flaked coconut
1 cup sugar
1/3 cup flour
1/4 tsp. salt
4 egg whites
1 tsp. almond extract
1/2 tsp. grated orange peel
1/2 tsp. grated lemon peel
1 cup chopped almonds

Mix together coconut, sugar, flour, and salt. Whip egg white to soft peak and add to coconut mixture. Stir in almond extract, lemon and orange peel, and nuts. Drop teaspoon sized cookies onto ungreased cookie sheet about 2 inches apart. Bake at 325 degrees for 20 minutes or until edges are golden. Cool. Serve.

June 30, 1929
Dear Hannah,

We had the lovliest spring this year, but southern summer has definitely reared its ugly head! It has been hot, sticky and suffocating every day for over two weeks! This kind of weather is hard on all of us, but especially Leona. Her stroke last fall left her partially paralyzed, and it has affected her speech so badly that she simply refuses to talk at all. Poor old dear. I never thought I would miss her voice, but now that I don't hear it at all, I feel strangely deprived.....or depraved, depending on how you look at it. I spend long hours in her room reading to her and writing letters for her. I can honestly say that I have grown to genuinely love the old bitty....and she me.

Julianna invited her fiance, Randall Quincy, to supper last evening. He is

Fabulous Fudge

Makes 8 doz. (death by chocolate)

2 cups chopped toasted walnuts, almonds or pecans
3/4 stick unsalted butter
3 cups sugar
1 1/2 sticks unsalted butter
5 oz. evaporated canned milk
12 oz. semi-sweet chocolate chips
10 oz. marshmallow cream
1 tsp. vanilla
1 tsp. almond extract

Toast nuts with 3/4 stick butter. Transfer to medium sized bowl. Grease 9X13 inch glass baking dish and chill in freezer. Stir sugar, remaining butter, and evaporated milk over low heat until sugar dissolves. Bring to boil, stirring constantly for 5 minutes. Remove from heat and stir in chocolate chips, marshmallow cream, and extracts. Mix in nuts. Spread in chilled baking dish. Chill to firm. Cut into 1 inch squares. Serve. Yum!

Grandma's Chocolate Toffee

Makes 1 pound (sweet and chewy)

1 cup butter
1 1/2 cups sugar
1/2 tsp. baking soda
6 oz. semi-sweet chocolate chips
3/4 cup chopped pecans
1 tsp. vanilla

Stir butter and sugar over low heat until sugar dissolves. Simmer (covered) for 3 minutes. Uncover and continue cooking, stirring occasionally, until mixture reaches 290 degrees on candy thermometer. Remove from heat and quickly stir in soda. Pour evenly onto greased cookie sheet. Spread chocolate chips over entire surface. Sprinkle with nuts. Chill 2 hours. Cut into 1 inch squares. Serve.

a seminary student and is the nicest young man. He is gentle and soft spoken like Julianna. Oh, how she adores him. Randall is quite a musician and after supper the two young people went out onto the veranda to enjoy what cool the evening could provide. Randall had brought along his mandolin and proceeded to play several secular songs. Julianna sang along with that marvelous soprano voice of hers. Soon Amanda joined them.... and then Franklin. They were all singing together, improvising harmony as they went along. The sound of their voices was sweet in the stillness of the evening. Leona's bedroom is at the far corner of the house with the window facing the avenue and a sidelong view of the veranda. When I entered her room, I could tell that she was straining to listen to the goings-on outside, so I positioned her

Chocolate Dipped Strawberries

Makes 2 doz. (show stopper!)

1/2 pound white chocolate plus 1 tbl. shortening
2 oz. semi-sweet chocolate plus 1 tbl. shortening
24 lg. fresh strawberries with stems
1/2 pound ground nuts

Line cookie sheet with wax paper. Wash and pat dry strawberries. Melt white chocolate over low heat. In separate pan, melt semi-sweet chocolate over low heat. Working quickly, hold strawberry by stem and gently dip 3/4 of berry into white chocolate. Remove and hold 5 seconds to slightly set. Dip half of berry into semi-sweet chocolate. Roll berry lightly in nuts and set on prepared cookie sheet. Repeat process for all remaining berries. Wow!

Double Chocolate Peanut Clusters

Makes 7 doz. (deliciously deadly!)

2 pounds white chocolate
3 pounds semi-sweet chocolate
24 oz. dry roasted peanuts

Melt chocolates over low heat, stirring constantly. Remove from heat. Stir in peanuts. Drop by teaspoons full onto wax paper. Cool to set.

Chocolate Nut Pralines

Makes 5 doz. (wonderful!)

7 cups whipping cream
4 cups sugar
2 cups finely chopped nuts (almonds, pecans, or walnuts)
3 tbl. unsweetened cocoa powder

Who says I say all those things they say I say?

at the window where she could see the veranda. I sat down beside her. We listened to the music and I hummed along quietly to myself. Either the song-ster's moods changed, or they ran out of silly songs to sing, because it got very quiet for a few minutes. Then Randall began to play Amazing Grace, my most favorite of all hymns. Soon my family's voices, blended in harmony, filled the night. Leona reached for my hand and squeezed. I will remember forever the look of perfect peace on her stroke ravaged face. What a brave old soul she is.

Amanda, the bane and boon of my existence, has been expelled from school! It seems as though she, in her typical fashion, has once again managed to commit verbal suicide. Evidently, a school chum was being victimized by several of the older girls. Priscilla and Amanda have been friends since they

Chocolate Nut Pralines (cont.)

Cook cream and sugar over low heat to dissolve sugar. Increase heat and bring to boil. Reduce heat and cook to "soft ball" stage on candy thermometer. Mix in nuts. Remove from heat and stir to cool slightly. Add cocoa and stir. Spoon candy onto wax paper (tablespoon size). Cool.

Nutty Chocolate Truffles

Makes 3 doz.

8 oz. semi-sweet chocolate
1/2 cup whipping cream
1/4 stick butter
3/4 cup powdered sugar
3 egg yolks
1 tsp. rum extract
1/2 cup ground nuts

Heat chocolate, cream, and butter over low heat. Add sugar and yolks. Whisk until smooth. Remove from heat and add extract and nuts. Pour into glass baking dish and chill until cool enough to mold. Shape into small bite sized balls and roll in nuts. Refrigerate and continue to harden. Serve.

Creamy Cheese Truffles

Makes 4 doz.

1/2 cup sugar
8 oz. cream cheese (softened)
6 oz. unsweetened chocolate
1 tsp. vanilla
1 tsp. honey
cocoa
ground almonds

Beat together sugar and cream cheese. Melt together chocolate and honey. Add to cheese mixture. Stir. Add vanilla. Mix well. Shape into bite-sized balls. Roll in nuts and cocoa. Chill.

were babies. The fact that Priscilla is Jewish never bothered Amanda in the least. As it shouldn't. Priscilla, however, has not had her sorrows to seek. I suppose when one's friend is being attacked, you are obliged to take charge of the situation, but did she have to get into a fist fight? It gets worse. It seems that Amanda and Priscilla ended up in a tangled pile of flying fists and feet. Pay attention, Hannah, the best is yet to come. When the School Mistress arrived on the scene and demanded an explanation, all fingers pointed to Priscilla. The obviously distraught mistress made the unfortunate comment that Jews should not be allowed to attend the school in the first place. To that remark, my Amanda shouted, "You are a miserable old bigoted bat"...then hit her. Now I am in the position to punish Amanda for physi-

Perfect Peanut Butter Fudge

Makes 2 doz. (disgustingly healthy!)

3 cups crunchy peanut butter
1 cup powdered milk (dry)
1 cup raisins
2/3 cup sesame seeds
1/3 cup honey
3 tbl. wheat germ

Combine all ingredients together, mixing thoroughly. Mixture will be thick and sticky. Press into 8 inch baking pan. Chill. Cut into squares. Store in refrigerator.

Gottahavit Now! Peanut Brittle

Makes 1 pound

1 cup sugar
1/2 cup light corn syrup
1 cup roasted peanuts
1/4 stick butter
1 tsp. vanilla
1 tsp. baking soda

Cook sugar and syrup until sugar dissolves and mixture begins to turn golden. Stir in peanuts, butter, and vanilla. Bring to boil. Remove from heat and pour onto greased cookie sheet, spreading evenly. Cool. Break brittle into large pieces. Serve.

Applettes

Makes 1 doz. (a must!)

2/3 cup applesauce
3 packets unflavored gelatin
2 cups sugar
2/3 cup applesauce
1 cup chopped walnuts
1 tsp. vanilla

cal violence and insolence, but yet praise her for her values! Honestly, this child drives me crazy! How do you ever manage with all your brood?

Enough for now. Hugs and kisses to all of yours. Emily

1 tsp. cinnamon
1/4 tsp. lemon juice
powdered sugar

Mix 2/3 cup applesauce with gelatin. Let stand 10 minutes. Add remaining applesauce, cinnamon, and sugar. Cook over low heat to simmer for 5 minutes. Remove from heat. Add nuts, lemon juice, and vanilla. Stir to blend. Pour evenly into powdered sugar dusted glass 8 inch square baking dish. Dust generously with powdered sugar. Chill. Cut into 1 inch squares.

Note: For Cotlettes, substitute apricot sauce for applesauce.

Many a man who misses his anniversary catches it later.

PIES
TARTS
&
CHEESECAKES

PIE TALK

Want your pies to look like they belong on a magazine cover? When you have put the pie "together", but before you scallop the edges of the crust, cup you hands and gently press around the inside edge of the pastry to form an indentation between the edge of the pie and the center. A slight mound will form in the pie giving definition to your work of art. Brush the top crust with melted butter and sprinkle with sugar before baking for a finished product with a golden "even colored" look. Don't forget to put at least three slits in the top crust. One to let the pie "breathe", and two more "cause your mamma did it that way".

TART TALK

Tarts can be more fun than you can imagine. Fill them with anything .... mousse topped with whipped cream, pudding topped with meringue, fruit filling topped with ice cream, cheesecake topped with fresh fruit ... just about anything will do, and oh what delicious and attractive surprises you can create. I have even been known to fill a tart shell with thick stew and serve it with salad....Yum! You'll find lots of recipes in this book that will be just perfect for a "tart filling". Have fun!

CHEESECAKE TALK

Cheesecakes can be tricky, but the key to this marvelous dessert is to make sure each step in mixing produces a smooth and creamy texture. Bake cheesecakes until golden and still moist...never brown and crumbly. Always store cheesecakes in refrigerator (covered). Remember cheesecakes are always best served fresh, but most freeze well.

NOTES

Hannah's Perfect Pie Crust

Makes 2 (9 inch) Crusts

Stop being afraid of, and frustrated with, pie crust! This crust is easy to make and produces a light flaky textured pie crust every time. It's easy! Using the right shortening is the secret. **Use a high quality pure vegetable shortening.** If you use the best, you will create the best.

3 cups flour
1 1/3 cup shortening
1 tsp. salt
1 small egg
1 tsp. vinegar
1/4 cup COLD water

Combine flour and salt. Cut in shortening. Put about a half cup of the mixture into your hand and squeeze. Mixture should just barely hold together. Too moist? Add a little flour. Too dry? Add a little shortening. Beat egg and shake together with 2 tablespoons water and vinegar. Add egg mixture to flour mixture. Stir to blend. Add remaining water 1 tablespoon at a time, mixing with hands until dough is moist and holds together easily. Dough should be a little sticky, but not gooey. Divide dough in half and form into 2 large balls. Place ball betweeen two large sheets of waxed paper. Flatten slightly. Begin to roll out dough using short shaping motions. Continue to roll out dough until shaped into about a 12 inch diameter round. Remove top layer of waxed paper. Place dough upside down in pie pan and remove remaining waxed paper. Edges should drape over sides of pan. Fill crust with pie filling and repeat for top. When top is in place, trim edges to allow only 1/2 inch overlap. Flute edges. Slit top of crust with knife in creative pattern to allow pie to "breathe" while cooking. Bake according to pie instructions.

Single Pie Crust: Cut recipe in half.
Pre-baked Pie Shells: Pierce bottom and sides of un-cooked shell with fork thoroughly to allow crust to "breathe" while baking.

A beautiful girl is even more beautiful when she is laughing.

Tasty Mini-Tarts:

For delicious cream and fruit tarts, prepare Hannah's Perfect Pie Crust (two crust recipe). Roll out dough to about 1/4 inch thick and cut into 5 inch diameter rounds. Carefully mold rounds over the bottoms of muffin tin cups. When neatly in place, pierce pastry bottoms with fork two or three times to allow pastry to "breathe" while baking. Bake cups at 350 degrees until lightly golden. Do not over bake. Cool. Gently remove pastry cups from tins. (Cups should pop off with a little upward pressure. This may take a little practice....... be patient.) Serve pastry cups fresh or freeze for later use.

Fill cups with fruit pie filling, mousse, or pudding and top with whipped cream, ice cream, sauce, meringue or anything that strikes your fancy. Be creative!

Prefect Fruit Pies:

The secret to terrific fruit pies is to cook the filling before you bake the pie. I can't begin to tell you how many times I have baked a lovely, tasty fruit pie that is perfect in every way except that there is a gap the size of the Grand Canyon between the filling and the top crust. Therefore, cook the filling first to reduce the risk of monumental fruit shrinkage while baking. In addition, I have found that if I freeze my prepared pies before baking, then bake them semi-frozen (very slowly), my pies are evenly golden and super flakey. Also, this method allows you to prepare several pies in advance, having a fresh fruit pie available for "emergency" desserts, any time you wish. Try it. I think you will be pleased with the results! P.S.: Don't forget the ice cream. What's fruit pie without ice cream!

Never mind the Joneses. I'm trying to keep up with the Waltons.

July 4, 1931
Dear Emily,

Ruth left for Kenya today. It gives a totally new meaning to "Independence Day". Andrew and I put her on the train to New York this morning and I had the sickening feeling that I would never see her again. I know that I can be melodramatic, but Emily.......Kenya! Actually, Africa needs Ruth. If nothing else the children in the missionary school will learn to laugh and they certainly will never be bored. Isn't this the girl that had to be dragged to church every Sunday? And isn't this the same teenager that said, "There is no God!"? Well she must have changed her mind.....or God changed it for her. Let me tell you something, Emily. That blond, gorgeous, 21 year old that I put on the train this morning, believes in God! Her face was the vision of peace and her will

Fresh Apple Pie

Makes one 9 inch deep dish pie

8 cups sliced tart apples (peeled)
1 1/4 cup sugar
2 tbl. water
4 tbl. flour
4 tbl. butter
1 1/2 tsp. cinnamon
1 tsp. nutmeg
1/2 tsp. allspice
1/2 tsp. salt

Combine sugar and butter. Cook over low heat until butter melts and mixture begins to bubble. Add flour and stir to blend. Add water gradually and stir to blend. Add apples and cook uncovered until thick and apples are nearly tender. Do not over cook. Add spices and salt. Stir to blend. Cool. Make crust and fill. Sprinkle top of pie with sugar. Bake at 425 degrees for 15 minutes. Reduce heat and bake at 325 degrees for 45 minutes or until evenly golden. Or try freezing pie before baking.

Fresh Blueberry Pie

Makes one 9 inch pie

8 cups fresh blueberries
1 cup sugar
2 tbl. flour
4 tbl. water
3 tbl. butter
1/2 tsp. salt
2 tbl. lemon juice
1/2 tsp. cinnamon

God made woman beautiful so man would love her .... and then he made her foolish so she would love man.

never stronger. Her two years of bible and language school were wonderful for her. I still remember the day she sat with me at the kitchen table and told me about her decision to become a missionary. I thought, anyone but Ruth. God knows our hearts better than we do. Bless you as you go, my dear Ruth. God will be by your side as He has always been by mine.

Clare is happy in her new home. I'm so glad she and Bob decided to stay in Montana. Why is it that the rest of you find it necessary to move to the other side of the world? You, Emily, in South Carolina, Augusta in San Francisco, Beth in Texas, and now, Ruth to Africa. Thank goodness Mary Ella is finally coming home. She has taken a teaching position in a small town near here. Just a one room school house but I'm sure she will be happy.

Combine sugar and butter. Cook over low heat until butter melts and mixture begins to bubble. Add flour gradually and stir to blend. Add water gradually. Stir to blend. Add berries and cook uncovered until mixture is thick and berries are nearly tender. Add lemon juice, salt, and cinnamon. Cool. Prepare crust and fill. Sprinkle top crust with sugar. Bake at 425 degrees for 15 minutes. Reduce heat to 325 degrees and bake until evenly golden. Cool and serve.

Fresh Cherry Pie

Makes one 9 inch pie

7 cups fresh pitted cherries
1 cup sugar
3 tbl. butter
2 tbl. flour
1/2 cup water
1 tsp. lemon juice
1 tsp. cinnamon
dash of nutmeg
1/2 tsp. salt

Combine sugar and butter and cook over low heat until butter is melted and mixture begins to bubble. Add flour and stir to blend. Gradually add water. Add cherries and cook until cherries are just barely tender. Add lemon juice, nutmeg, and cinnamon. Cool. Prepare and fill crust. Sprinkle top crust with sugar. Bake at 425 degrees for 15 minutes. Reduce heat to 325 degrees and bake 45 minutes or until evenly golden. Cool and serve.

When you quit having birthdays .... you're dead!

We are still struggling to keep hold of the ranch. The boys are a big help to Andrew even though they are still pretty young. It seems like we just get through one financial crisis and another is scratching at the back door. But we will survive. It will take a lot more than the depression to push us off our land. We are in a lot better shape than most. It's so sad to see people losing everything they have ever worked for.

A.J. and Patrick are growing like weeds. A.J. is quiet like his Dad and Patrick is happy go lucky...always looking on the bright side. Bless his heart .

Beth and Richard are going to stay in Texas. They are better off there. Richard's ranch is on family land and he doesn't have to worry about losing it. Beth loves Texas and I know she is happy. I miss her, but she has to live her own life.......just like she

Fresh Huckleberry-Peach Pie

Makes one 9 inch pie

4 cups fresh huckleberries or tart blackberries
4 cups fresh peaches (peeled and sliced)
1 1/2 cups sugar
2 tbl. flour
3 tbl. butter
1 tsp. cinnamon
1/2 tsp. salt

Combine sugar and butter and cook over low heat until mixture bubbles. Add flour and stir to blend. Gradually add water. Add peaches and berries. Stir to blend. Cook until mixture thickens and fruit is just barely tender. Add spices and salt. Cool. Prepare crust and fill. Sprinkle top crust with sugar. Bake at 425 degrees for 15 minutes. Reduce heat to 325 degrees and bake 45 minutes, or until evenly golden. Cool. Serve.

Fresh Rhubarb-Strawberry Pie

Makes one 9 inch pie

5 cups fresh rhubarb (chopped)
5 cups fresh strawberries (sliced)
2 cups sugar
4 tbl. flour
2 tbl. water
3 tbl. butter
1 tsp. grated orange peel
1 tsp. cinnamon
1 tsp. all spice
1/2 tsp. salt
dash nutmeg

The only reason that some brides promise to love, honor, and obey is that they don't want to start an argument in front of all those people.

always has.

As for Andrew and me, it's funny, we have never had less, but on the other hand, we have never been happier. It has been years since we actually worked side by side. We are really enjoying each other. It doesn't seem possible that we have been married almost 29 years. You know Emily, I was looking at him the other day, and he is actually better looking now than he was when we got married. Wish I could say the same for me. Why is it that men get better as they get older and women just get older? Doesn't seem fair does it? Why am I asking you. I can't even get you to admit that you ever reached 30! You vain thing.

Oh, I almost forgot to tell you! Douglas Far-thington has moved back here. Wasn't he sweet on you once? Or were you sweet on him? Anyway,

Fresh Rhubarb-Strawberry Pie (cont.)

Combine sugar and butter and cook over low heat until mixture bubbles. Add flour. Stir to blend. Add water and rhubarb. Cook until mixture is thick and rhubarb is tender. Add spices, orange rind, and salt. Remove from heat and fold in strawberries. Cool. Prepare crust and fill. Sprinkle sugar over top crust. Bake at 425 degrees for 15 minutes. Reduce heat to 325 degrees and bake 45 minutes or until evenly golden. Cool and serve.

Sour Cream Pumpkin Chiffon Pie

Makes one 9 inch pie (light and lovely)

1 1/2 cups canned pumpkin
3/4 cup brown sugar
1/3 cup whipping cream
2 egg yolks
1 envelope unflavored gelatin
1 tsp. cinnamon
2 tsp. pumpkin pie spice
1/2 tsp. salt
1/2 cup sour cream
1 tsp. vanilla
2 egg whites
1/3 cup sugar
pinch of salt
1/4 tsp. cream of tartar
pre-baked pie shell

Second, third, and fourth babies are not nearly as breakable as the first.

talk about getting better with age! He took over the family ranch when his dad died last spring. We had him over to dinner Sunday after church and he had the boys on the edge of their chairs with stories of all the places he has been. He was a mining engineer and traveled everywhere with his work. Really an interesting fellow.

All for now.
Love from all of us,
Hannah

Pie shell:
Use recipe for Hannah's Perfect Pie Crust (pre-baked shell)

Pie Filling:
Combine pumpkin, sugar, cream, egg yolks, gelatin, spices, and salt. Cook over low heat to just below boil. Do not boil. Add sour cream and vanilla. Cool. Chill. Beat egg whites with a pinch of salt until soft peaks form. Add cream of tartar. Add 1/3 cup sugar (gradually) . Whip until stiff. Fold into pumpkin mixture. Pour into prepared crust and chill several hours (covered). Serve with whipped cream topping.

Simple Buttermilk & Raisin Pie

Makes one 9 inch pie

1 cup sour cream
1 cup sugar
2 eggs
2 tbl. vinegar
1 tsp. cinnamon
1/2 tsp. cloves
1/2 tsp. nutmeg
1 cup raisins
unbaked pie shell

Pie Shell:
Use recipe for Hannah's Perfect Pie Crust (unbaked shell).

Mix all ingredients together (except raisins) and beat 1 minute. Add raisins. Pour into prepared unbaked pie shell. Bake at 425 degrees for 15 minutes. Reduce heat to 325 degrees and bake 45 minutes or until golden. Cool. Cut into individual slices. Top with Buttermilk Sauce. Serve.

Why is it that the bride always looks stunning and the bridegroom just looks stunned?

Buttermilk Sauce:
1 cup buttermilk
3 tbl. whipping cream
1/2 tsp. cornstarch
1 tsp. cinnamon
dash nutmeg
3 eggs
1/2 cup sugar

Combine first 5 ingredients and cook over low heat until boiling, stirring constantly (mixture may appear curdled). Beat eggs and sugar until fluffy and pale. Add to cooked mixture. Return to heat and stir to thicken. Serve warm over pie.

Banana Cream Custard Pie

Makes one 9 inch pie

3 cups milk
4 egg yolks (beaten)
2/3 cup sugar
1/4 cup cornstarch
1/2 tsp. salt
8 oz. cream cheese
1 tsp. vanilla
1 tbl. butter
1/2 cup finely chopped nuts
2 large bananas (sliced)
1 cup shredded coconut (toasted)
pre-baked pie shell

Pie Shell:
Use recipe for Hannah's Perfect Pie Crust (pre-baked shell).
Combine milk, eggs, sugar, salt, and cornstarch and cook over low heat. Bring to boil. Add cream cheese and stir until melted. Remove from heat. Add nuts, vanilla, and butter. Stir to blend. Cool. Place bananas in bottom of pie shell. Top with custard mixture. Sprinkle with coconut. Chill. Serve.

February 28, 1932
Dear Hannah,

You and your "convenient amnesia"! Don't try and fool me Hannah, you were as sweet on Douglas Farthington as I was. For that matter, all the girls were. You were always swooning over his "sea green eyes"! You disgusting girl. And by the way, I still haven't forgiven you for the "Strawberry Cobbler" incident. Don't play dumb. You always said that you had nothing to do with it, but I know better. There isn't another person on earth devious enough to think up such a terrible plot. Why I ever trusted you to make that donation to the church baked goods auction for me I'll never know. What a hateful thing to do .... using 2 cups of salt instead of 2 cups of sugar. Now thirty years later, I want to know how you arranged for

Honey Cheese Pie

Makes one 9 inch pie

Pie Shell:
1 1/2 cups flour
1/2 cup sugar
1 tsp. cinnamon
1/2 tsp. nutmeg
1/2 tsp. baking powder
1/2 tsp. salt
1/3 cup butter
1 egg (beaten)

Combine first 6 ingredients. Cut in butter. Add eggs. Mix well. Add more flour if dough seems too soft. Form into ball. Chill 1 hour. Roll out dough and place in buttered 9 inch pie pan. Flute edges. Chill.

Filling:
1 1/4 lbs. ricotta cheese
3/4 cup sugar
1 tsp. cinnamon
1 cup honey
4 beaten eggs

Beat cheese until fluffy. Add sugar and eggs. Beat 2 minutes. Add honey and cinnamon. Beat 2 minutes. Pour filling into shell. Bake at 350 degrees until firm (about 50 minutes). Cool. Sprinkle pie with cinnamon. Top with whipped cream and lace with chocolate sauce if desired. Serve.

Saying yes to a child is like blowing up a balloon .... you have to know when to stop.

Douglas to buy that infamous cobbler! Remember how it was? The person that made the dessert had to share it with the person who bought the dessert. I still flush at the mere memory. The look on his face! You miserable wretch ..... I could have killed you. When I told Franklin the "cobbler story" at supper tonight he nearly laughed himself into convulsions. And then there was the time at the Harvest Festival Dance that you stole the last bloom of the season off my mother's prize winning rose bush. The last time I saw that rose was in your teeth as you glided across the dance floor doing some silly imitation with Douglas. I still can't believe you told mother that I picked that yellow rose and gave it to you! You scoundrel!

No real news to tell here. Franklin's business is surviving the depression, just barely. I have cut

Heavenly Pie

Makes one 9 inch pie

1 1/2 cups sugar
1/4 tsp. cream of tartar
4 egg whites
3 tbl. shredded coconut
1 pint whipping cream
4 egg yolks
3 tbl. lemon juice
1 tbl. grated lemon rind
1/8 tsp. salt
12 whole fresh strawberries

Combine 1 cup sugar and cream of tartar. Beat egg whites to soft peak. Gradually add sugar mixture. Beat until very stiff glossy peaks form. Spread mixture into well greased 9 inch glass pie pan, making bottom 1/4 inch thick. Sprinkle rim with coconut. Bake 1 hour at 275 degrees. Cool.

Beat egg yolks over low heat. Stir in remaining sugar, lemon juice, lemon rind, and salt. Cook slowly, stirring constantly, until mixture thickens. Cool. Whip 1 cup whipping cream and fold into mixture. Pour custard into meringue shell. Chill 12 hours. Top with unsweetened whipping cream. Garnish edges with strawberries.

Lime Souffle Pie

Makes one 10 inch pie

7 egg yolks
7 egg whites
3/4 cup sweetened condensed milk
3/4 cup lime juice
2 tsp. grated lime peel
1/4 tsp. salt
1 drop green food coloring
1 package unflavored gelatin
2 tbl. water

1/2 cup sugar
1/8 tsp. cream of tartar
1 1/2 cups whipping cream
2 tbl. powdered sugar
pre-baked 10 inch pie crust

Stir egg yolks, 1/2 cup condensed milk, and lime juice over low heat until mixture begins to thicken. Stir in lime peel, salt, and food coloring. Remove from heat. Combine gelatin and water. Let stand 10 minutes. Add remaining condensed milk. Stir mixture over low heat until gelatin dissolves. Do not allow to boil. Add gelatin to yolk mixture. Beat egg whites to soft peak. Add cream of tartar. Add sugar slowly and beat until stiff. Fold into yolk mixture. Pour filling into crust and bake at 350 degrees for 15 minutes or until edges begin to brown. Cool. Chill. Whip whipping cream with powdered sugar and spread over pie. Garnish with very thin lime slices. Serve.

Mom's Best Lemon Meringue Pie

Makes one 9 inch pie

1 1/2 cups sugar
1 1/2 cups water
1/2 tsp. salt
1/2 cup cornstarch
1/3 cup water
4 egg yolks (beaten)
1/2 cup lemon juice
3 tbl. butter
pre-baked pie shell

Pie Shell:
Use Hannah's Perfect Pie Crust (pre-baked shell).

corners until there aren't any more to cut. And we are just "making do" with everything we can. We are doing without everything but happiness. Franklin (Mr. Sunshine), always has something happy to say and refuses to be "depressed". Bless his heart.

Goodbye for now, dear. I'll write again soon.
Love, Emily

Mom's Best Lemon Meringue Pie (cont.)

Combine sugar, 1 1/2 cups water, and salt . Cook over medium heat until boiling. Mix cornstarch and 1/3 cup water to make smooth paste. Add to boiling mixture gradually, stirring constantly. Cook until thick and clear. Remove from heat. Cool slightly. Combine egg yolks and lemon juice. Gradually stir into thickened mixture. Return to heat and cook until mixture bubbles, stirring constantly. Remove from heat. Stir in butter. Cool to lukewarm (covered). Fill pie shell.

Meringue:
4 egg whites
dash of salt
1/2 tsp. cream of tartar
1/2 cup sugar

Combine egg whites and salt. Beat until soft peaks form. Add cream of tartar and sugar, 1 tablespoon at a time. Beat until very stiff. Heap onto pie smoothing meringue all the way to edges, mounding toward center. Using spatula, form several sweeping peaks. Bake at 375 degrees until golden. Be careful, burns easily.

When a youngster hears a bad word it usually goes in one ear and out his mouth.

Butterscotch Meringue Pie

Makes one 9 inch pie

Use Hannah's Perfect Pie Crust (single pre-baked), Butterscotch Pudding recipe, and Meringue recipe.

Chocolate Meringue Pie

Makes one 9 inch pie

Use Hannah's Perfect Pie Crust (single pre-baked), Chocolate Pudding recipe, and Meringue recipe.

Coconut Meringue Pie

Makes one 9 inch pie

Use Hannah's Perfect Pie Crust (single pre-baked), Coconut Pudding Recipe, and Meringue recipe.

Peanut Butter Cream Pie

Makes one 9 inch pie (peanut butter lovers dream)

Nut Crust:
1 1/2 cups finely chopped peanuts
1/2 cup sugar
1/3 cup butter
1/4 tsp. allspice

Mix together and press into 9 inch glass pie pan. Freeze.

Peanut Butter Cheese Filling:
1 1/4 cups whipping cream
1 1/2 cups powdered sugar
2 tbl. vanilla
8 oz. cream cheese (softened)
1 cup creamy peanut butter
2 tbl. butter

Beat cream and 1/4 cup sugar to soft peak. Combine remaining sugar, cheese, peanut butter, vanilla, and butter. Beat until fluffy. Fold in cream mixture. Pour into crust. Chill. Top with Hannah's Hot Fudge just before serving.

August 9, 1933

Dear Em,

  We have had a tremendous summer. The apple and pear trees have never been heavier with fruit, the garden produced and produced until I could hardly keep up with it, and it seemed like the barn yard came alive with baby "everything" this year. Even my old, nasty tempered sow, Pork Chop, had 14 piglets! Thinking of that pig reminds me to tell you about our almost unfortunate "Chase Race" last Sunday.

  Clare, Bob and the boys were over for Sunday dinner. I guess it was about 3:00 when all the commotion started. The adults were sitting on the porch enjoying the afternoon. Rob was playing with the dog and supposedly watching Davey, who just turned three in July. I was totally engrossed in a story that Andrew was telling when all of a

Double Layer Chocolate-Mocha Pie

Makes one 10 inch pie (be still my heart!)

Pie Shell: (pre-baked)
Use Hannah's Perfect Pie Crust

Filling: Layer One
8 oz cream cheese (softened)
1/2 cup sugar
1/2 cup powdered sugar
1 stick butter
4 tbl. unsweetened cocoa
1 tsp. instant coffee (dry)
1 tsp. vanilla

Blend cream cheese, sugars, butter, cocoa powder, coffee and vanilla. Spread in bottom of pie shell. Chill.

More Filling: Layer Two
1 tbl. unflavored gelatin
1/3 cup orange juice (hot)
1 1/4 cups whipping cream
5 eggs
1/2 cup sugar
1 tbl. unsweetened cocoa
1 tsp. vanilla
1/2 cup grated semi-sweet chocolate

Combine gelatin and juice. Stir. Let stand 5 minutes or until gelatin is dissolved. Beat cream to soft peaks. Beat eggs, sugar, cocoa, and vanilla. Add gelatin mixture to egg mixture and beat 1 minute. Fold in whipped cream. Chill until mixture begins to set. Pour into pie shell. Chill to firm. Sprinkle with grated chocolate. Serve.

The closest to perfection anyone ever comes is when he writes his resume.

70

sudden we heard a crash, a scream, and a squeal. The sound had come from the barn so we jumped up and rounded the east side of the house just in time to see Davey running as fast as his chubby little legs could carry him with Pork Chop right behind him, gaining ground with every step. My heart stopped! Bob was off the porch first, running to intercept child and pig. He managed to snatch Davey just ahead of Pork Chop. Well, let me tell you Emily, it took an hour before we all caught our breath, Davey calmed down, and the pig was securely back in her pen. Then Andrew took the child up onto his lap to ask him what had happened. Davey had evidently been teasing Pork Chop and her babies. I guess Pork Chop figured enough was enough and just came right through the pen after him. The rest is history, but Davey's explanation of how "pig

Peachy Peach Cobbler

Serves 8

Filling:
4 lbs. thick sliced peaches (peeled)
1 1/2 cups sugar
1 tsp. cinnamon
dash nutmeg

Combine all ingredients and let stand in refrigerator (covered) over night.

Pastry:
Use Hannah's Perfect Pie Crust recipe for full pie. Roll out one ball of dough in rectangular shape and cut into 10 (1 inch wide) long strips. Repeat with remaining dough and set aside. Pour filling into bottom of well buttered 9 X 13 baking dish. Thin slice one stick butter and dot over filling. Sprinkle with 2 tbl. sugar. Lay 10 pastry strips over filling (all in same direction) and trim edges. Bake at 350 degrees for 20 minutes. Remove from oven. Lay 10 pastry strips in opposite direction and trim edges. Continue baking until golden brown. Cool slightly. Serve with vanilla ice cream.

Easy Mini-Cheesecakes

Makes 12 (perfect for lunches and picnics)

12 vanilla wafers
16 oz. softened cream cheese
2/3 cup sugar
1 tsp. vanilla
2 eggs

Mix cream cheese, sugar, vanilla, and eggs until well blended and pale in color.

Line muffin tins with foil cupcake liners. Place one vanilla wafer in each cup. Fill cups 3/4 full with cheese mixture. Bake at 325 degrees for 25 minutes or until golden. Remove from pan when cool and top with jelly, preserves, fruit, chocolate, or cinnamon. Be creative!

chased boy" is the best. Davey said, "Well, I said blah blah piggy and then she said blah blah Davey and then here she come." Kids. How they ever manage to live long enough to grow up is a mystery to me.

I got a wonderful letter from Ruth last week. She just loves Kenya. There are 37 students in the missionary school now and she is really enjoying teaching. The way she describes the country side, you would think it was paradise, though the thought of living so near dangerous animals and snakes does bother her some. But all in all she manages pretty well. She doesn't sound the least bit homesick. It appears Ruth has found her niche in life. I'm truly happy for her, but I miss her terribly.

Augusta's new baby girl sounds just precious. How I wish I could see her, but the odds that I

"No Time to Waste" Cheesecake

Makes one 9 inch pie (a snap!)

1 prepared graham cracker pie crust
1 (8-oz.) package softened cream cheese
14 oz. sweetened condensed milk (not evaporated milk!)
1/3 cup lemon juice
1 tsp. vanilla
1 quart fresh or frozen whole strawberries
1 1/2 cups sour cream mixed with 1 tbl. sugar

Mix first 4 ingredients until smooth. Pour into pie shell. Chill. Cover with sour cream mixture. Decorate with strawberries. Serve.

"The Purist's" Cheesecake

Makes one 8 inch cake (no frills, just the real thing)

Crust:
2 cups graham cracker crumbs
1 cup sugar
1/2 cup brown sugar
1/2 cup melted butter
1 tsp. cinnamon

Mix all ingredients together until blended. Press evenly into well greased 8 inch glass pie plate or 8 inch spring form pan.

Filling:
5 (8-oz.) packages cream cheese (softened)
7 egg yolks
7 egg whites
1 1/2 cups sugar
1 tsp. vanilla
pinch of salt
2 1/2 cups sour cream
6 tbl. flour
Beat yolks, sugar, cream cheese, vanilla and salt. Add sour cream and flour and beat until smooth. Using perfectly clean utensils, beat egg whites and cream of tartar in glass

will ever be able to travel
to San Francisco are just
about zero...it might as
well be Mars. You know
what she named her?
Emily Kay! Don't get a
puffed head.

Well, my dear, I must
close for now. My love to
all.
Hannah

bowl until stiff. Fold into cheese mixture. Pour into pie shell. Bake at 325 degrees for 1 hour. Turn off oven. Let cake stand in oven for 1 additional hour (keep door closed). Cover and chill.

Rum Raisin Cheesecake

Makes one 8 inch cake (rich and oh so mellow)

2 cups graham cracker crumbs
3 tbl. sugar
2 1/2 tbl. butter
5 (8-oz.) packages softened cream cheese
1 1/2 cups sugar
1 1/2 tbl. vanilla
7 egg yolks
7 egg whites
2 tsp. rum extract
1/3 cups half and half
1 cup raisins

Mix crumbs, sugar, and butter. Grease 8 inch glass pie plate or 8 inch spring form pan. Press crumb mixture evenly into plate.

Beat cheese until smooth. Add sugar, vanilla, and egg yolks. Beat well. Beat egg whites to soft peak and add to cheese mixture. Blend well. Mix in rum extract and half and half. Stir in raisins. Pour into pie shell. Place cheesecake into shallow pan of water and bake at 350 degrees for 90 minutes, or until cake feels dry to the touch. Cool. Chill. Serve.

Most of us can forgive and forget ..... we just don't want the other person to forget what we forgave.

73

White Chocolate-Cherry Cheesecake

Makes one 10 inch cake (heavenly!)

Success is relative ....
the more success the
more relatives.

Crust:

1 1/2 cups finely crushed shortbread cookie crumbs
1/2 cup ground walnuts
3 tbl. sugar
1/4 tsp almond extract
4 tbl. melted butter

Combine all ingredients until well blended. Press evenly into well greased 10 inch glass pie plate or 10 inch spring form pan. Bake 10 minutes at 350 degrees. Cool.

Filling:

8 oz. white chocolate (chopped)
4 (8 oz.) packages softened cream cheese
1 cup sour cream
6 eggs
1 cup sugar
4 tbl. flour
1 tsp. vanilla
1/4 tsp almond extract

Melt chocolate in double boiler. Cool to lukewarm. Beat cheese and sour cream. Add eggs, sugar, vanilla, and almond extract. Gradually beat in flour. Stir chocolate and cheese mixture together. Pour filling into crust. Bake at 325 degrees for 40 minutes (filling will be firm at edges but still soft in center). Cool on rack. Chill.

Glaze:

8 tbl. whipping cream
8 oz. white chocolate
1/4 cup cherry preserves (melted)

Melt chocolate in whipping cream until smooth. Remove from heat. Add melted preserves, folding in gently. Spoon over cheesecake and serve.

Chocolate Marble Cheesecake

Makes one 10 inch cake (chocolate lover's delight)

Love is like a mush-room. You never know if it's the real thing until it's too late.

Crust:
2 cups chocolate cookie crumbs
1/2 cup unsalted butter (melted)
4 tbl. dark brown sugar
1 tbl. unsweetened cocoa
1/4 tsp. cinnamon.
Combine all ingredients and press evenly into bottom of 10 inch spring form pan.

Filling:
5 oz. semi-sweet chocolate finely chopped
1 oz. unsweetened chocolate finely chopped
5 (8-oz.) packages softened cream cheese
1 cup sugar
2 tbl flour
6 eggs
1/3 cup whipping cream
1 tsp. vanilla
Melt chocolates together in double boiler. Cool to luke-warm. Beat cheese, sugar, and flour until smooth. Beat in eggs. Stir in cream and vanilla. Pour 1/3 batter into chocolate and mix well. Pour 1/2 of remaining plain batter into crust. Pour chocolate batter over first layer. Pour remaining plain batter over chocolate layer. Swirl gently with thin knife to marble. Do not over swirl. Bake at 425 degrees for 15 minutes. Reduce heat and bake additional 50 minutes or until firm in center. While baking prepare topping.

Topping:
2 cups sour cream
1/4 cup sugar
1 tsp. vanilla
Mix all ingredients together and pour over hot, baked cheese cake. Bake at 350 degrees until set. Cool and chill.

Glaze:
1 cup whipping cream
7 oz. semi-sweet chocolate
Simmer ingredients together until smooth. Do not boil. Cool. Remove cheesecake from pan onto serving plate. Pour glaze over cake so that it runs over sides. Chill and serve. Garnish with whipped cream and single fresh strawberry per serving. Magnificent!

PUDDINGS
MOUSSE
&
PASTRY

PUDDING AND MOUSSE TALK

What wonderful desserts, pie fillings, and treats these make! These recipes leave you lots of room to be creative. I know you will find several family favorites. Cooking slowly and evenly is the key here. A thick, creamy pudding, mousse or custard is the direct result of low heat, stirring consistency, and attentiveness. (In other words, don't try to talk on the phone and wash the dog while you are cooking custard of any kind.) Store creations in refrigerator, tightly covered with plastic wrap, after they are completely cooled.

WAFFLE TALK

Waffles can be a "happening". Use them for breakfasts, lunches, dinners and even desserts. The days of waffles as "something on which you throw butter and maple syrup" are over! Don't over cook them. Waffles should be light and moist, not hard and brown with the texture of a frisbee. Some waffles can even be prepared ahead of time, stored in plastic bags, frozen, and reheated in the micro-wave!

NOTES

November 12, 1936
Dear Hannah,

I was thinking of you today on your birthday....your 50th, I might add. You still think you are some sort of spring chicken, no doubt. A half a century, Hannah. Doesn't that bother you at all? I'm absolutely dreading my birthday in July. I guess 50 is only significant when you are 49.

This has been a busy and emotional year for me, Hannah. I was just sitting here by the fire wondering what else could possibly happen in the Sawyer household in 1936.

Amanda's wedding was pleasantly uneventful. What a relief. I never know what will happen from one moment to the next with that girl. I have to admit that she was the lovliest bride I have ever seen. Her ivory colored dress shocked everyone but

Dark Chocolate Cream Pudding

Serves 8

(bittersweet and smooth)

1 1/2 cups sugar
1 tsp. salt
6 tbl. cornstarch
1 cup unsweetened cocoa
3 cups evaporated milk
3 cups water
3 eggs (beaten)
3 tbl. butter
2 tbl. vanilla

Combine sugar, salt, cornstarch, and cocoa in large sauce pan. Add milk, water, and egg. Cook over low heat, stirring constantly until mixture thickens. Remove from heat and add vanilla and butter. Stir to blend. Cool. Serve.

Butterscotch Cream Pudding

Serves 8

1 1/2 cups dark brown sugar
1 tsp. salt
6 tbl. cornstarch
3 cups evaporated milk
3 cups water
3 eggs (slightly beaten)
3 tbl. butter
2 tbl. vanilla

Cook sugar, salt, cornstarch, milk, water, and eggs over low heat until thickened, stirring constantly. Remove from heat. Add butter and vanilla. Stir to blend. Cool. Serve.

Is there life after birth?

76

me. After all, I raised this headstrong creature. She just couldn't be persuaded into white, no matter what I said. I can't really blame her. She looks simply "dead" in white. That red hair and white skin were never meant to be wrapped in something so colorless. She was magnificent in ivory and walked down the aisle on her father's arm with an air that dared anyone to defy her. Sound familiar?

Randall accepted a post in a church in Philadelphia and he and Julianna moved there in May. I'm sure they will love it. Philadelphia is such a beautiful city. I will miss Julianna. She has been such a wonderful companion.... more like a friend than a daughter.

I miss Leona, Hannah. She taught me so very much over the years. Especially patience toward the end. She suffered for such a long time and never

Coconut Cream Pudding

Serves 8

1 1/2 cups sugar
1 tsp. salt
6 tbl. cornstarch
3 cups evaporated milk
3 cups water
3 eggs (slightly beaten)
2 tbl. butter
2 tbl. vanilla
1 cup shredded coconut

Cook sugar, salt, cornstarch, milk, water, and eggs over low heat, stirring constantly. When mixture thickens, remove from heat and add vanilla, butter, and coconut. Stir to blend. Cool. Serve.

Country Fudge Bread Pudding

Serves 8 (a real country favorite)

2 cups half and half cream
10 oz. semi-sweet chocolate
1/2 cup butter
1/2 cup sugar
3 eggs (beaten)
2 tsp. vanilla
6 slices white bread (1/2 inch cubes)

Combine cream, chocolate, butter and sugar. Cook over low heat, stirring constantly, until ingredients melt and blend. Whisk in eggs and vanilla. Stir in bread. Pour into 1 1/2 quart baking dish. Place in large pan with 2 inches hot water (add more water as needed). Bake at 325 degrees for about 40 minutes or until firm in center. Serve warm.

Tired of wrinkles? Iron your face.

really complained. If I loved her for nothing else, it was for that lesson.

My life is changing so rapidly that it makes my head spin. You know that change has never been easy for me. Is the world moving faster or is it my imagination? This letter even sounds like a rushed inspiration of sporatic thought.

The depression has certainly left its mark among our friends and neighbors. Who would have ever thought that something like this could happen in a great country like ours. But then I suppose nations are like people...they are allowed their ups and downs too. Speaking of depression....I certainly seem to be just that as I re-read this letter. I was thinking the other day that I am still, after all these years, homesick for Montana. Isn't that the silliest thing? After all, I'm nearly "you know

Vanilla Meringue Pudding

Serves 6

2 cups milk
2 tbl. butter
8 tbl. sugar
2 1/2 cups white bread crumbs
2 egg yolks (beaten)
3/4 cup jam (your choice!)
2 egg whites
pinch of salt
1/4 tsp. cream of tartar

Heat milk, 2 tbl. sugar, and butter over low heat almost to boiling. Pour milk over bread crumbs. Stir in yolks. Pour into well buttered 1 qt. oval baking dish. Bake at 350 degrees until firm (about 20 minutes). Remove pudding from oven and spread jam over top. Beat whites and salt until soft peaks form. Add cream of tartar and 5 tbl. sugar (gradually). Beat until stiff. Mound meringue over pudding. Sprinkle with remaining sugar. Bake at 275 degrees for 25 minutes or until golden. Serve hot.

Steamed Coconut Chocolate Ginger Pudding

Makes 10 servings

4 oz. semi-sweet chocolate
1/4 cup butter
1/2 cup unsweetened canned coconut cream
3 egg yolks (slightly beaten)
1 tbl. vanilla
1/3 cup vanilla cookie crumbs
2/3 cup gingersnap cookie crumbs
3/4 cup flaked coconut
1/4 tsp. ground ginger
1/2 cup dark brown sugar
1/4 cup flour
1 tsp. baking powder

what!" But then, it wouldn't matter how old I was, the memory of the everlasting youth and freshness of Montana will always be a part of me.

At any rate, my dearest Hannah, I hope your 50th birthday was a memorable and joyful occasion. I'm sure it was. You wouldn't know how to have a birthday that wasn't. Bless you dear heart.

Love to Andrew and the boys.
Missing you, Emily

Coconut Chocolate-Ginger Pudding (cont.)

3 egg whites
1/8 tsp. salt
2 tbl. sugar
1/4 tsp. cream of tarter

Melt chocolate and butter over low heat. Remove from heat and whisk in coconut cream, vanilla, and egg yolks. Add cookie crumbs, coconut, brown sugar, flour, ginger, and baking powder. Stir to blend. Beat whites and 1/8 tsp salt to soft peak. Add cream of tartar and gradually add sugar. Beat until stiff. Fold into batter. Pour batter into well buttered jello mold or individual molds. Place in large pan with 3 inches of water (add more water as needed). Simmer, tightly covered, until pudding is firm (about 2 hours). Cool 5 minutes. Invert mold onto serving plate and remove pudding. Cover with Sour Cream Sauce. Serve warm. Marvelous!

Sour Cream Sauce

Makes 1 cup

3/4 cup whipping cream
3 tbl. powdered sugar
3 tbl. sour cream
1 1/2 tsp. vanilla

Whip cream and sugar to soft peak. Fold in sour cream and vanilla. Serve.

The trouble with kids is that when they are not being a lump in the throat they are being a pain in the neck!

Old-fashioned Date Toffee Pudding

Serves 8

1 cup flour
1/2 tsp. baking powder
2 tbl. butter (softened)
7 tbl. white sugar
1 egg (beaten)
1/2 cup boiling water
3 oz. pitted dates (finely chopped)
1/2 tsp. baking soda
1 tsp. vanilla
1 1/2 cups whipping cream
3/4 cup butter
1/2 cup dark brown sugar

Combine flour and baking powder. Cream 2 tbl. butter with white sugar. Stir in egg and flour mixture. Stir to blend. Pour boiling water over dates. Blend in baking soda and vanilla. Stir into batter. Pour into well buttered 6 X 8 inch baking pan. Bake at 375 degrees for 35 to 40 minutes or until firm. Cool 5 minutes. Turn out onto serving plate and cover with toffee sauce.

Toffee Sauce:
Combine cream, butter and dark sugar. Cook over low heat until thickened, stirring constantly. Remove from heat. Pour over pudding. Serve warm.

Emily's Orange Sponge Pudding

Serves 6

3/4 cup butter (softened)
3/4 cup sugar
3 eggs
1 tbl. grated orange peel
2 tbl. orange juice
1 1/3 cups flour
1 tsp. baking powder

Cream butter until fluffy. Add sugar. Blend well. Add eggs and beat 2 minutes. Stir in orange juice and peel. Fold in flour and baking powder. Pour into well buttered mold. Place in large pan with 3 inches of water (add more water as needed). Simmer, tightly covered, until pudding tests firm (about 90 minutes). Let cool 15 minutes and turn out of pan onto platter. Cover with Cinnamon Sauce, if desired.

Cinnamon Sauce
Makes 1 1/2 cups

1 1/2 cups milk
4 eggs
1/3 cup sugar
1 tsp. vanilla
1 1/2 tsp. cinnamon

Heat milk over low heat. Beat eggs and sugar until pale. Gradually beat in hot milk. Return to heat and cook to thicken. Do not boil. Remove from heat and add vanilla and cinnamon. Serve hot.

"So Simple" Chocolate Mousse

Serves 6 (a quick and easy dessert)

2 1/2 cups semi-sweet chocolate chips
2 tsp vanilla
pinch of salt
2 cups whipping cream (heated to boiling point)
7 egg yolks
2 egg whites
pinch cream of tartar

When choosing between two evils ..... choose the one you have never tried before.

To err is human ..... to blame it on someone else is humaner.

October 2, 1939
Dear Emily,

Don't be such a worry wart, Em. A. J. will be fine! He is just another one of the Hansen children with infectious wanderlust. A.J. was never meant to be a rancher, or a farmer, or a "stay at home" anything. I'm convinced that he was born with a head full of far away places. And even though it breaks my heart to see him leave, the navy was really his only choice. There is no future here for a young man like A.J., looking for adventure. Emily, I learned a long time ago that to try and confine my children in the name of protection is a cruel love indeed. He goes with my blessing...and my heartache. Without my blessing <u>his</u> heart would ache. I love him too much for that.

Would you like to hear some good news? My darling Mary Ella is to be married on the 10th of

"So Simple" Chocolate Mousse (cont.)

Combine chocolate, vanilla, and salt in blender. Chop. Add hot cream and blend 30 seconds on medium speed. Add yolks and blend 10 seconds. Pour into bowl and cool. Whip egg whites, using perfectly clean untensils, and cream of tartar until stiff. Fold into chocolate mixture. Pour into individual cups for serving and chill. Top with whipped cream if desired.

Quick Mocha Mousse

Makes 6 servings (a touch of coffee)

2 tsp. instant coffee
2 tsp. vanilla
3 1/2 cups whipping cream
1 1/4 cups powdered sugar
1 cup unsweetened cocoa
pinch of salt

Dissolve coffee in vanilla. Add cream, sugar, cocoa, and salt. Beat to soft peaks. Spoon into individual serving bowls and chill. Top with whipped cream and pinch of cocoa powder if desired.

Orange-Chocolate Mousse

Serves 6

8 oz. semi-sweet chocolate
1 3/4 cups sugar
4 tbl frozen orange concentrate
3 tsp. grated orange peel
7 egg yolks (beaten)
7 egg whites
1 1/4 cup whipping cream

Face it....out of the mouths of babes come words you shouldn't have said in the first place.

82

Melt chocolate in double boiler. Add 1 cup sugar. Stir to dissolve. Blend in orange juice and orange peel. Stir in yolks. Cool. In clean bowl, whip egg whites to soft peak. Continue beating and add sugar 1/4 cup at a time. Beat until stiff. Fold into chocolate mixture. Whip cream and fold into mixture. Spoon into individual serving dishes and chill. Garnish with sprinkle of cinnamon.

Frozen Caramel Mousse

Serves 6 (old-fashioned flavor)

Mousse:
1/8 cup water
1 cup light brown sugar
3/4 cup sugar
5 egg yolks
2 cups whipping cream
1 tsp. vanilla

Combine sugar and water and boil until sugar completely dissolves. Beat yolks until pale. Gradually pour in sugar mixture and continue beating until mixture begins to cool. Beat whipping cream and vanilla to soft peak. Fold into caramel mixture. Pour into individual servings. Cover and freeze.

Sauce:
1/3 cup dark brown sugar
1/3 cup sugar
1/2 cup whipping cream
3 tbl. butter
pinch of salt
1/2 tsp. vanilla

Simmer all ingredients (except vanilla) for 5 minutes to blend flavors and dissolve sugar. Let cool. Add vanilla and stir to blend. Spoon sauce over mousse and serve immediately.

June. I thought she would never do it. After all, she was 35 last April. She always said that teaching was her life, and her students her children. I guess she wasn't planning on Stewart Parker waltzing in and sweeping her off her feet. He is a widower with 3 beautiful children (that just adore Mary Ella, I might add). The way he looks at her, Em! You would think she was the only woman in the world! I'm sure she will be gloriously happy.

Patrick is 16! Can you believe it? What a handsome young man he is. He looks so much like my father that sometimes the resemblance literally stuns me. He is still a happy-go-lucky character with a hilarious sense of humor. That child simply cripples me with laughter regularly. He loves being here on the ranch. He doesn't particularly like ranching, but the country surroundings seem

Summer Strawberry Mousse

Serves 8 (fresh and light)

2 1/2 cups fresh strawberries (hulled and pureed)
2/3 cup sugar
1/4 tsp. salt
4 tbl. warm water
2 tsp. lemon juice
1 1/4 oz. envelope unflavored gelatin
2 egg yolks
2 egg whites
2/3 cup sugar
2 tbl. honey
1 1/4 cup whipping cream
8 whole strawberries
whipped cream

Heat strawberries, 2/3 cup sugar, and salt until sugar dissolves. Combine water, lemon juice, and gelatin until gelatin dissolves. Stir into strawberry mixture. Cool. Beat yolks in double boiler. Add remaining sugar and honey, and stir to thicken. Remove from heat. Add 1/4 cup of strawberry mixture. Stir to blend. Pour remaining egg mixture into remaining strawberry mixture. Stir. Whip 1 cup cream and fold into above mixture. In clean bowl, beat egg whites to soft peak. Fold into mixture. Spoon into individual serving cups. Cover and chill. Garnish with whipped cream and one whole strawberry.

Luscious Lemon Mousse

Serves 10 (rich and lemony)

7 egg yolks
7 whole eggs
2 cups sugar
1 1/4 cups lemon juice
3 tbl grated lemon peel
pinch of salt
2 sticks chilled butter (chunked)

1 cup chilled whipping cream
2 cups fresh or frozen berries (your choice)
4 tbl. sugar

Beat together eggs and yolks, sugar, lemon juice, peel, and salt. Stir over low heat until thickened. Remove from heat and stir in butter. Blend well. Whip cream to soft peaks. Fold into lemon mixture. Spoon into individual servings. Chill. Mash berries. Add remaining sugar. Taste for sweetness. Cover and chill. Pour over mousse just before serving.

Crispy Cookie Cups

Makes 20 cups (the perfect serving cup)

1 1/2 cups flour
1 cup powdered sugar
4 egg whites (lightly whipped)
4 egg yolks (lightly whipped)
2 tsp grated lemon rind
1 tbl honey

Blend sugar, flour, and lemon rind. Add egg yolks and honey. Stir. Add egg whites. Mix well. Let stand 30 minutes. Grease a cookie sheet and mark as many 5 inch circles as will fit within sheet. Drop one tsp. of batter into each circle and spread batter to fill circle. Bake at 350 degrees for 4-5 minutes or until cookies are brown at edges but still soft in center. Working quickly, remove cookies one at a time with a wide spatula and gently mold around the bottom side of muffin tin cups. Cool. Remove from tins. Repeat process until all batter is used.

Note: This recipe may take a little practice, but it's worth it!

Some people cause happiness wherever they go... others whenever they go.

The bravest person of all: The person who discovered frog legs were edible!

January 28, 1940
Dear Hannah,

I am writing with bad news. Franklin has had a mild heart attack. The doctors do not seem to be overly concerned, though they do insist that he retire immediately. He is forbidden any unnecessary physical activity or excitement. Franklin has always been such an active man that this sudden immobilizing would be devastating. For that reason he has decided to continue living like he always has.....at top speed.

I was hysterical over this decision at first, but then Franklin took me by the hand and walked me out onto the veranda. We sat in the swing that he gave me so many years ago and he poured out his inner most thoughts, fears and desires. His life has been so very full. If he could live it all over again, he would change nothing...not one moment. He wants to

Belgian Waffles

Makes 12

2 tbl. dry yeast
1/4 cup lukewarm water
1 tsp. sugar

Dissolve together and set aside to activate.

1 3/4 cups warm water
2 cups canned evaporated milk
8 egg yolks
8 egg whites
1 tsp. vanilla
1 tsp. almond extract
5 cups flour
1 tsp. salt
2 tbl. sugar
1 cup melted butter

Beat egg yolks and add yeast mixture. Add vanilla, almond extract, and milk. Combine flour, sugar, and salt. Add to egg mixture gradually, stirring to blend. Stir in melted butter until mixture is smooth. Beat egg whites until stiff and fold into batter. Let stand in warm place for 45 minutes or until doubled. Cook waffles in belgian waffle iron. Use 1 cup batter per waffle.

Best Bran Waffles

Makes 4

3/4 cup flour
1/2 cup all bran cereal
1 tsp. baking powder
1/4 tsp. salt
1 tbl. sugar
1/2 cup milk (warm)
1 egg
2 tbl. vegetable oil

live the remainder of his life surrounded by laughter and newness. He wants to swim with his grandsons, argue with his daughter, take long walks with me, and continue to run his business. If his life is shorter because of this, he is ready to accept it.

As for me, I have shed many tears. The thought of life without him terrifies me, but I am adopting your philosophy, Hannah. To confine him in the name of protection would indeed be a cruel love. For that reason, I will thank God for every day that is allowed my husband.
Love, Emily

Best Bran Waffles (cont.)

Beat together milk, oil, sugar, and all bran. Cool. Add egg. Beat to blend. Add salt, baking powder, and flour. Blend until smooth. Use batter as directed for individual waffle maker.

Healthy Oat Waffles

Makes 6

3 egg yolks
3 egg whites
3/4 cup warm water
1/3 cup vegetable oil
1 tbl. honey
1 cup oat germ
1/2 cup oat flour
1 tsp. sugar

Beat yolks, water, oil, and honey. Stir in oat germ and oat flour. Beat egg whites and sugar until stiff. Fold into batter. Use batter as directed for individual waffle irons.

Maple Wheat Waffles

Makes 6

2 cups milk
1/3 cup melted butter
1/3 cup maple syrup
2 egg yolks
2 egg whites
1 cup flour
3/4 cup whole wheat flour
1/2 cup buckwheat flour
1 tbl. baking powder
1 tsp. salt
1/2 tsp. cinnamon
1/4 tsp. baking soda
1/4 tsp. cream of tartar
1 tbl. sugar

Maple Wheat Waffles (cont.)

Combine milk, butter, syrup and yolks. Blend. Add flours, baking soda, baking powder, cinnamon, and salt. Stir to blend. Beat egg whites until foamy. Add 1 tbl. sugar and cream of tartar and beat until stiff. Fold into batter. Use batter as directed for individual waffle irons.

Make something wonderful for dinner .... reservations.

Herb Yogurt Waffles
Makes 4

1 cup plain yogurt
4 eggs separated
1/3 cup melted butter
1 1/4 cup flour
1 tsp. parsley
1 tsp. thyme
1/2 tsp. coriander
1 tsp. baking soda
1/2 tsp. salt
dash of pepper
1/8 tsp. cream of tartar
1 tbl. sugar

Combine yogurt, yolks, and butter. Blend. Add flour, seasonings, and baking soda. Blend until smooth. Beat whites to soft peak. Add sugar and cream of tarter and beat until stiff. Fold into batter. Use batter as directed for individual waffle irons.

Gingerbread Waffles
Makes 4

1/3 cup brown sugar
2 egg yolks
2 egg whites
1/2 cup milk plus 1 tsp. vinegar
1/4 cup molasses
3 tbl. butter (melted)
1 cup flour

1 1/2 tsp. baking powder
1 1/2 tsp. ground ginger
1/2 tsp. cinnamon
dash of nutmeg
1 tsp. baking soda
1/4 tsp. salt
1 tsp. sugar
1/8 tsp. cream of tartar

Combine milk and vinegar. Let stand 10 minutes. Combine brown sugar, yolks, molasses, and butter. Beat 1 minute. Add milk mixture. Blend. Add flour, baking powder, spices, baking soda, and salt. Beat 1 minute. Beat egg whites and salt until soft peak. Add 1 tsp. sugar and cream of tartar and beat until stiff. Fold into batter. Use batter as directed for indiviual waffle iron.

Caribbean Waffles

Makes 6

3/4 cup shredded coconut (toasted)
1 cup milk
1 tbl. lime juice
4 tbl. melted butter
2 egg yolks
2 egg whites
1 tsp. grated orange peel
1 tsp. grated lemon peel
1 tsp. vanilla
1/4 tsp. rum extract
1 1/4 cups flour
1/2 tsp. baking powder
1/2 tsp. baking soda
pinch of salt
pinch of cream of tartar
2 tbl. sugar
1/2 cup canned crushed pineapple (well drained)

Children may tear up the house, but they never break up a home.

Christmas 1941
Dear Emily,
    My Christmas wish this year is for world peace and that my son did not have to die in vain. The shock of A.J.'s death is still as cold. My only refuge is that he died being where he wanted to be, doing what he wanted to do, and being whom he was. I pray for all the mothers who lost their sons. All the wives who lost their husbands. And all the children who will never know their fathers. It is unbelievable that America is at war.

    Andrew, is inconsolable. I have watched this man march through life taking whatever was his lot with command and determination. But A. J.'s death has taken the spark completely out of him. He is drained ...emotionally spent. I pray every day that God will heal his broken heart. I wish there was a way for me to take

Caribbean Waffles (cont.)

Combine milk and lime juice. Let stand 10 minutes. Beat butter, yolks, peels, and extracts for 1 minute. Add flour, coconut, baking powder, and baking soda. Stir to blend. Beat whites, and salt until soft peak. Add sugar and cream of tartar and beat until firm. Fold into batter. Use batter as directed for individual waffle irons.

Fudge Dessert Waffles

Makes 6

2 oz. unsweetened chocolate
1/2 stick butter
3 eggs
2/3 cup sugar
1 tsp. vanilla
1 cup buttermilk
1 1/4 cup flour
1/2 tsp. baking powder
1/2 tsp. baking soda
1/2 tsp. salt
dash nutmeg
dash allspice
3 oz. semi-sweet chocolate (chopped)

Melt unsweetened chocolate and butter over low heat. Cool. Beat eggs, sugar, and vanilla. Add buttermilk and stir to blend. Add flour, baking soda, baking powder, salt, and spices. Mix well. Fold in chopped chocolate. Stir. Use batter as directed for individual waffle irons.

Hannah's Danish Pastry

Makes 2 1/2 doz. (rich, flakey, melt in your mouth)

2 tbl. dry yeast
1/4 cup lukewarm water
1 tsp. sugar

him away from here for awhile. Remove him from the memories.

The rest of the family is dealing with their loss as they can. Pray for us,
Em.
Love, Hannah

Dissolve together and set aside to activate.

4 cups flour
1/2 cup sugar
1 cup butter flavored shortening
1 cup dry powdered milk
1 tsp. salt
2 cups warm water
2 eggs (beaten)
1 tsp. vanilla
1/2 cup melted butter
1/2 cup brown sugar
1/2 cup white sugar
1/2 cup raisins
2 tbl. cinnamon

Combine flour, sugar, salt, and (dry) powdered milk. Cut in shortening. Add eggs, water, vanilla and yeast mixture. Stir lightly, just to moisten. Cover and chill 2 hours. Roll out dough onto floured surface into large rectangle shape 1/2 inch thick. Spread melted butter over entire surface of dough. Combine brown and white sugar, raisins, and cinnamon. Sprinkle over surface. Carefully roll dough lengthwise into large jelly roll. Cut roll into 1 inch sections and place on ungreased cookie sheets about 1 inch apart. Flatten each roll slightly with fingers to seal layers together, tucking trailing edge under. Cover and let raise 20 minutes in warm area. Bake at 350 degrees for 10-15 minutes or until filling bubbles and rolls are slightly golden. Cool 5 minutes and frost.

Icing:
1 cup powdered sugar
1 tsp. vanilla
1 tbl. butter
milk

February 17, 1942
Dearest Hannah,

My heart goes out to you. No one really knows how you must feel, but know that I love you and I am here, always, if you need me.

Pearl Harbor is a disaster that will remain a scar on this country forever, as it will the hearts of those that lost loved ones. God be with you and Andrew, Hannah. We will all pray for peace.

Love, Emily and Franklin

Combine sugar, butter, and vanilla and add enough milk to make icing syrupy. Lace icing over rolls sparingly. (For a rich creamy addition, top with cream cheese topping.)

Cream Cheese Topping:
8 oz. softened cream cheese
2 tbl. powdered sugar
1/3 cup sour cream
1 tsp. vanilla
Blend all ingredients together until smooth. Whip 2 minutes. Spread over rolls when ready to serve and top with fresh berries.

Spicy Sugar Puffs

Makes 2 doz.

3/4 cup lukewarm water
1 tbl. yeast
1/4 cup sugar
1/4 cup softened butter
1 tsp. salt
1 1/2 cups flour
1 egg
1/2 cup melted butter
3/4 cup sugar plus 2 tbl. cinnamon

Dissolve yeast in water along with a pinch of sugar. Add sugar, salt and 1/2 of the flour. Beat 2 minutes until smooth. Add egg and shortening. Beat in remaining flour until smooth. Grease muffin tins and fill cups half full with dough. Cover, place in warm area, and let rise until double in volume. Bake 15-20 minutes at 375 degrees. Turn out of tins. Roll tops in melted butter, then roll in sugar and cinnamon mixture. Serve warm with hot cocoa.

Misery is a woman with a live secret and a dead telephone.

Yummy Yogurt Scones

Makes 12

3 cups flour
3 tbl. sugar
1 tsp. baking powder
1 stick softened butter
2 egg yolks (beaten)
1 1/2 cups plain yogurt
2 egg whites mixed with 2 tbl. water

Combine flour, sugar, and baking powder. Cut in butter. Add yolks and yogurt. Stir to blend. Knead dough on floured surface lightly. Roll out 1/2 inch thick and cut in 2 inch rounds. Place on cookie sheet and brush with egg white mixture. Bake at 400 degrees until golden (about 20 minutes). Serve hot with jam and tea.

Raised Donuts

Makes 12

1 cup milk
3/4 cup sugar
1 tsp. salt
1/3 cup shortening
1 package dry yeast
2 eggs (beaten)
4-5 cups flour

Scald milk and pour over sugar, salt, and shortening. Stir to blend. Cool to lukewarm. Add yeast. Stir lightly. Let stand 5 minutes. Add eggs. Stir. Add 4 cups flour, 1 cup at a time. Stir to smooth. Mixture should be thick and sticky. Knead in remaining flour until smooth and firm but not dry. Return to bowl. Cover and let rise until double in bulk. Roll out dough on floured surface 2/3 inch thick. Cut with donut cutter. Place on lightly greased cookie sheet and let rise again. Fry in very hot oil until golden. Drain and dip tops in sugar, powdered sugar, or cinnamon. Or, if you like, frost with your favorite frosting and sprinkle with nuts or coconut.

Cake Donuts

Makes 12

2 1/2 tbl. shortening
3/4 cup sugar
2 eggs
1 cup milk
3-4 cups flour
3 tsp. baking powder
1 tsp. salt
1 tsp. allspice

Mix together shortening, sugar, and eggs. Add milk and spices. Add flour 1 cup at a time, until dough is firm but not dry. Roll out onto floured surface and cut with donut cutter. Fry in very hot oil until golden brown. Drain and frost or leave plain.

Happiness is like honey...you can't spread even a little without getting some on you.

Applesauce Fritters

Makes 3 doz.

4 eggs
2 cups sugar
1 tsp. vanilla
4 tbl. vegetable oil
4 tsp. baking powder
2 tsp. baking soda
2 cups applesauce
2 cups buttermilk
1 tsp. salt
2 tsp. allspice
2 tsp. cinnamon
8 cups flour

Mix eggs, sugar, vanilla, and oil together. Add applesauce and buttermilk. Stir to blend. Add remaining ingredients. Mix well. Drop tablespoon sized fritter dough into very hot oil and fry until golden brown. Drain. Dust with powdered sugar and cinnamon. Serve.

SOUPS
SALADS
&
SANDWICHES

SOUP TALK

Who isn't warmed by the very thought of a big pot of simmering soup, on a cold snowy day? Keep soup stock ready to use in the freezer, then add your imagination to make delicious homemade soups and stews. My husband accuses me of making "refrigerator soup"..... adding "selected" leftovers to prepared soup stock. I prefer to call it magic. At any rate, he always manages to lick the platter clean and ask for more. Try it. It is magic!

SALAD TALK

Crunch a bunch of munchable veggies! Fresh vegetables are one of the delights of my life. I must confess that I have to have adult supervision when I am working in the garden, since I do more "grazing" than weeding. Salads are such great fun! Wash veggies in cold water, gently pat dry, place them in a metal bowl (covered) and refrigerate for a few minutes before making your salad extravaganza. The result....crisp, juicy vegetables. Oh! And try this trick. Place a small saucer in the bottom of your salad bowl. The excess dressing will drain to the bottom of the bowl leaving your salad fresher longer.

SANDWICH TALK

How could the Earl of Sandwich in 1750 ever have known that when he shoved a chunk of meat between two slabs of bread, for a portable lunch, he had created the "big deal meal"! .... We've come a long way, Earl. Sandwiches, nowadays, can be anything between two slices of bread (preferably homemade). Here's a hint for making a great sandwich. Need a traveling sandwich? Butter and freeze the bread slices. Then build your sandwich between the frozen slices. Sandwich will stay fresher longer.

NOTES

July 18, 1943

Dear Hannah,

Your letter was as welcome as the flowers in May. So you think you are the only one that can make a fool of yourself. Not so.

The following lesson in humility should only be shared with someone who truly appreciates the human ability to make a fool of one's self....and who enjoys a good laugh. Therefore, I am sharing this with you!

Picture, if you will, a "slightly" over weight, "slightly" over 50, woman in her bath robe, at 7:00 A.M. on a Saturday morning. Now picture, if you will, a cat stuck in a tree yowling as if she were being murdered (the cat, incidently, was given to the woman by her youngest daughter). And picture the tree, located at the edge of the front yard next to the sidewalk. If the picture is clear, then you will have no trouble imagining 6

Sunday Supper Soup

Makes about 2 quarts (hearty!)

2 lbs. extra lean ground beef or venison
2 eggs slightly beaten
1/2 cup bread crumbs
1 tbl. parsley
1/2 tsp. salt
1 tsp. crushed garlic
evaporated milk to moisten
1/4 cup olive oil
1 large onion (chopped)
1/2 cup diced celery
1 tsp. oregano
1/2 tsp. basil
1 tbl. garlic powder
2 bay leaves
3 tbl. flour
salt and pepper to taste
2 cups sliced carrots
6 beef bouillon cubes
1 large can of stewed tomatoes (mashed)
3 cups water
1 cup white wine
1 cup parmesan cheese

Combine meat, eggs, bread, parsley, 1/2 tsp. salt, pinch of pepper, 1 tsp. crushed garlic, and milk. Mix well. Make small meatballs from mixture. In large soup pot, brown meat balls in oil. Remove meat balls and set aside. Add onions and celery and cook until onions are clear. Add flour and spices. Stir. Add carrots, tomatoes, water, wine, and bouillon cubes. Simmer 1 hour to blend spices and cook carrots. Add meat balls and simmer 30 minutes longer. Just before serving, gradually add cheese and stir to blend. Serve with thick slices of fresh bread and butter.

Children say the funniest things, and usually in front of the wrongest people.

neighbors and 2 firemen trying to get the woman out of the tree long after the cat has scampered down of its own accord. Franklin laughed. In fact, the entire neighborhood is laughing. Now who is wearing a paper bag over her head? You are the last person from which I would expect empathy...so I know you are laughing too.

All is well here except for this miserable rationing... and my "victory garden" has not been much of a victory. This horrible war! Isn't anyone going to stop that maniac! My heart aches for you, and so many people like you, who have lost loved ones in this chaos. I pray every day that today will be the last day of the war.

I got a lovely letter from Julianna last week. She says that she has been active with the USO in Philadelphia and is quite enjoying it. She and Randall are doing fine.

Cheesey Cheddar Chunky Chowder

Makes 1 1/2 quarts (thick, creamy, and filling)

1 1/2 cups diced potatoes
1 cup diced carrots
1/2 cup frozen peas
6 tbl. butter
1 large onion (finely chopped)
1 medium green pepper (finely chopped)
6 tbl. flour
1 tsp. garlic powder
1/2 tsp. salt
dash of pepper
1 tbl. chopped parsley
3 cups chicken broth
2 cups evaporated milk
2 cups grated sharp cheddar cheese
croutons

Steam potatoes, peas, and carrots until tender. Cook onion and green pepper in butter until onion turns clear. Add spices and flour. Stir until mixture bubbles. Gradually add broth and milk. Simmer to thicken, stirring constantly. Add cheese and stir to blend. Add vegetables and heat. Do not boil. Serve hot. Sprinkle with croutons.

Broccoli-Cauliflower Pasta Cheese Soup

Serves 4 (this recipe doubles easily)

3/4 cup chopped onion
2 tbl. vegetable oil or butter
3 cups chicken broth
4 oz. pasta (your choice)
1/2 cup chopped broccoli
1/2 cup chopped cauliflower
3 cups evaporated milk
1/4 tsp. garlic powder

Philadelphia is really "home" for them now. They have made lots of friends, and all the activities that go along with pastoring a church keeps them busy.

I must go for now. Franklin and I are going picnicking this afternoon and I haven't even started to pack our lunch. (My delightful little garden offered me two worm-eaten tomatoes to take along, but I declined.)
Love, Emily

Broccoli-Cauliflower Pasta Cheese Soup (cont.)

1/2 tsp salt
dash pepper
1/2 lb. grated sharp cheddar cheese

Steam vegetables until just barely tender and set aside. Cook and rinse pasta. Cook onion in oil until clear. Add vegetables and spices. Stir. Add broth and milk. Stir lightly. Add pasta and cheese. Heat to simmer. Do not boil. Serve hot.

Easy Mushroom Soup

Serves 4 (simple and delicious)

1/4 cup vegetable oil
1 medium onion (chopped)
1 garlic clove (crushed)
1 lb. mushrooms (sliced)
5 cups boiling water
3 chicken bouillon cubes
1/2 cup celery (chopped)
1 tsp. parsley
1 tsp. Italian seasoning
1 bay leaf
3 tbl. butter
4 tbl. flour
salt and pepper to taste

Heat oil in soup pot. Add onion and garlic and cook until onions are clear. Add mushrooms and simmer to release juices. Stir in water, bouillon cubes, celery, and seasonings. In sauce pan, melt butter. Add flour and stir to blend. When mixture bubbles, add 1 cup soup broth. Blend. Add mixture gradually to remaining soup mixture. Stir. Simmer to blend and thicken. Serve hot.

If you can sleep like a baby you don't have one.

Cream of Garlic Soup

Serves 8 (Don't let the title scare you. Delicious!)

6 tbl. butter
1/2 lb. diced ham
8 garlic cloves (chopped)
1 onion (chopped)
1 diced potato
7 cups water
5 chicken bouillon cubes
2 cups whipping cream
1 tsp. parsley
salt and pepper to taste

Cook first five ingredients until onions turn clear. Add water and bouillon. Simmer until potato is tender. Remove from heat. In blender, puree entire mixture. Return to heat and add cream and spices. Heat, but do not boil. Serve hot.

Cream of Celery Soup
(Same basic recipe as Cream of Garlic Soup. Replace garlic cloves with 1 cup chopped celery plus 1 tsp. garlic powder.)

Husbands are like an egg. If you keep them in hot water long enough, they will get hard boiled.

Old Fashioned Cream of Chicken Soup

Serves 8 (perfect for cold snowy days)

Chicken Stock:
6 pounds chicken
12 cups water
1 whole peeled onion
2 cloves
2 celery stalks
2 halved carrots
2 tsp. parsley
10 peppercorns
2 bay leaves
1 tsp. thyme

*Give inflation a little
more time ..... and a
wooden nickle will
cost a dime.*

Stock:
Bake chicken until tender, but not dry.   Skin and bone chicken.   Set aside. Scrape contents of bottom of baking pan into large pot. Add remaining ingredients to pot. Add skin and bones to pot and simmer 3 hours. Remove from heat and cool to lukewarm. Strain stock. Remove onion, celery, and carrots (discard the rest). Return to heat and boil until liquid is reduced to 3 cups of clear broth .

Soup:
1/4 cup olive oil
chicken from stock
onion from stock (minced)
celery from stock (minced)
carrots from stock (minced)
1/3 cup flour
3 1/2 cups milk
1 1/4 cups whipping cream
1 tbl white wine
Salt and pepper to taste

Cook onion and celery in butter. Add flour and stir to blend. Stir in stock. Bring to boil. Gradually stir in milk. Reduce to simmer. Dice chicken and add to mixture. Add remaining ingredients. Heat and serve.

Hannah's Harvest Soup & Dumplings

Serves 12 (satisfies the biggest appetite)

1 lg. can stewed tomatoes (mashed)
8 cups beef stock OR 8 cups water and 6 beef bouillon cubes
1/2 tsp. salt
dash pepper
6 tbl. olive oil
2 small eggplants (chopped)
2 large onions (chopped)

June 5, 1945
Dear Emily,

Hurrah! Hurrah!
The war is over! I realize
that this is no great news
by now, but I still find
myself dancing a little jig
at the mere thought. It's
over, Em. Nobody else has
to die. No more bombs
and madmen. No more, no
more, no more! Andrew
agrees with President
Truman, that this will be
the war to end all wars. I
hope both of these great men
are right.

Nothing else to say. I
just wanted to share my
happiness with you!
Love, Hannah

2 large green peppers (chopped)
2 small zucchini (chopped)
1 tsp. thyme
1 tsp. basil
1/2 tsp. oregano
2 cloves garlic (crushed)

Combine tomatoes, stock, salt, and pepper. Simmer. Heat oil and cook remaining ingredients until nearly tender. Add vegetable mixture to stock. Simmer 30 minutes.

Dumplings:
1/2 stick butter
2 small onions (minced)
4 tbl. parsley
6 slices white bread
4 oz. extra lean ground beef
3 eggs
salt and pepper to taste

Melt butter. Add onion and parsley. Cook until onions turn clear. Remove from heat. Soak bread in enough water to cover. Squeeze out excess water. Combine bread, meat, onion mixture, and egg in bowl. Season with salt and pepper. Mix well. Roll mixture into tablespoon sized balls and drop into soup. Simmer soup 20 minutes and serve.

Country Market Soup

8 servings (a real winner)

1/4 stick butter
1 carrot (chopped)
1 stalk celery (chopped)
1 large potato (diced)
1 small onion (chopped)
1/2 turnip (chopped)
4 cups water
2 tbl. barley
2 tbl. lentils

18-oz. can stewed tomatoes (mashed)
1 8-oz. can kidney beans
7 beef bouillon cubes
3 tsp. worcestershire sauce
2 1/2 tbl. Italian seasoning
2 tsp. parsley
1 tsp onion salt
2 bay leaves
1 (8-oz.) can corn (drained)

In soup pot, cook first 6 ingredients. Simmer lentils and barley in water for 10 minutes. Add lentil mixture to soup pot. Add remaining ingredients. Bring soup to boil. Reduce heat and simmer 30 minutes. Serve hot.

Garden Tomato Soup

8 servings (Lovely, this one!)

2 leeks (whites only, washed thoroughly and diced)
1 stick butter
2 lg. carrots (diced)
2 small parsnips (diced)
3 cloves garlic (crushed)
1 large potato (diced)
1/3 cup red wine
4 cups water
4 beef bouillon cubes
4 lbs. tomatoes (diced)
1 tbl. parsley
2 tbl. basil
3 tsp. tarragon
1/2 tsp. nutmeg
salt and pepper to taste

Cook leeks, carrots, parsnips, garlic, and potatoes in butter until tender. Add water, wine, and bouillon cubes. Simmer 10 minutes. Add tomatoes and spices. Simmer 15 minutes covered and 30 minutes uncovered. Serve hot with buttermilk biscuits and honey.

Honeymoon: The interval between the bridal toast and the burnt toast.

Eureka! Onion Soup

Serves 8 (the best I have ever found!)

4 tbl. butter
5 tsp. olive oil
4 large onions (cut in half and thinly sliced)
4 cloves garlic (crushed)
4 tsp. sugar
1/2 cup flour
8 cups beef stock
1 cup white wine
2 tsp. worcestershire sauce
1 tsp. parsley
1/4 tsp. sage
1/4 tsp. thyme
1/4 tsp. coriander
1/4 tsp. allspice

Saute' first four ingredients until onions turn clear. Add sugar and stir until onions turn golden. Add remaining ingredients and simmer 1 hour. Serve hot. Sprinkle with garlic croutons and parmesan cheese.

Glacier Salad

Seves 8 (tangy and refreshing!)

1/2 small onion
2 tbl. vinegar
3 tbl. spicy brown mustard
1 small egg
1/2 tsp. sugar
salt and pepper to taste
1 cup vegetable oil
1/2 pound bacon
1 large bunch romaine lettuce (torn to bite size)
1 small iceberg lettuce (torn to bite size)
1 cup cooked asparagus spears (cut to 1 inch size)
1 cup marinated artichoke hearts (halved)
5 oz. blue cheese

You can't buy happiness with money and you can't buy groceries with happiness..... so it all comes out about even.

June 22, 1946
Dear Emily,

Thank you for your letter. Yes, my dear, I will be all right. I am in good hands.

Emily, I could not believe what I was seeing. I was walking to the garden to do some weeding when I heard that sickening noise. I knew immediately what it was but refused to believe it. When I looked up I could see the tractor on its side out in the field...the engine still straining. I knew what I would find before I ever reached him. How could this have happened? My poor darling Andrew. My only hope is that God took him quickly, and that he didn't suffer. How much more am I to endure?

I awakened this morning at 4:30. The sun was just rising and I leaned against the window, pressing my forehead to the glass. I wanted to cry, but couldn't. Then all of a

Puree onion and vinegar. Pour into bowl. Beat in sugar, egg, salt, pepper and mustard. Gradually beat in oil until mixture thickens. Cook bacon until crispy. Drain and crumble. Mix together vegetables. Toss with dressing. Serve with Eureka Onion Soup, for a real luncheon hit!

Market Day Chicken-Lentil Salad

Serves 8

1 1/4 cups lentils
4 1/2 cups water
2 lg. garlic cloves
1 med. onion
1/4 cup olive oil
2 1/2 tbl. wine vinegar
3 tbl. orange juice
2 tsp. water
1 tsp. thyme
1 tsp. cilantro
1/2 tsp. basil
1/2 tsp. salt
dash of pepper
8 oz. cooked chicken breast (cubed to bite size)
3 tomatoes (chunked)
1 lg. red bell pepper (seeded, halved, and sliced thin)
4 cups chopped cooked broccoli
1/2 cup cooked corn kernels
2 large bunches romaine lettuce (torn to bite size)

Bring lentils and water to boil. Reduce heat and simmer until tender. Drain and cool. Puree garlic, onion, oil, vinegar, juice, water, salt, pepper, and spices. Combine chicken, lentils, and vegetables in large bowl. Toss with dressing mixture. Chill and serve.

sudden I was angry.....so very angry! "Lord, why Andrew? Why have you done this to me", I screamed. Filled with hurt and anger I trudged through the morning's chores, cursing the pain that consumed me beyond what I thought I could ever bare. My faithful Becca stood in her stall patiently waiting...ready to do her job of filling my empty bucket with milk. I sat down on the milk stool that Andrew had made for me years before. And then the tears came. I wept for Andrew and A.J. and Abby and myself. I leaned my face against Becca's massive side and let my grief and rage wash over me in a rush of self pity. My precious Becca stood quietly and let me pour out my agony. And then it was over. A peace had filled me...an indescribable peace. I knew at that moment, as I will for the rest of my life that I

Apple-Raisin Chicken Salad

Serves 6

Sweet Mustard Dressing:
3 tbl. cider vinegar
4 tbl. vegetable oil
2 tbl. mayonnaise
1 tsp. Dijon mustard
1/2 tsp. sugar
salt and pepper to taste

Combine ingredients together in blender and mix well.

Salad:
2 cups cooked cubed chicken
1 medium head green cabbage (shredded)
1 cup red cabbage (shredded)
2 red delicious apples (unpeeled and small cubed)
1 small green bell pepper (seeded and finely sliced)
2 green onions (diced)
1/2 cup raisins

Combine ingredients together and toss with dressing. Chill and serve.

Sweet and Sour Coleslaw

Serves 12

2 lbs. green cabbage (shredded)
3/4 cup sugar
1/3 cup vinegar
1 tsp. salt
1 cup whipping cream

Combine all ingredients in large bowl. Toss lightly. Chill and serve.

Who ever said, "Where there's smoke there's fire".... never owned a fireplace.

am but a small part of a big plan and that all things happen in their own time. We go through life taking so much for granted, all wrapped up in the tedium of day to day living. And then everything changes.. without warning. Oh, Emily, there was so much I didn't say to Andrew. I wondered.... did he know that I loved him more than life itself? Did he know that he filled my life with joy and meaning? Did he know that half of me was him? Of course he did.

Emily, I realize now that death is a part of living....that you cannot have one without the other. From this loss I will heal. Love, Hannah

Garden Spinach Salad

Serves 6

4 cups fresh spinach (torn to bite size)
1 cup cucumber (thinly sliced)
1/3 cup sliced radishes
1/4 cup chopped green onion
2 hard boiled eggs (sliced)
1/2 lb. bacon (cooked, drained, crumbled)
1/2 cup pinion nuts (shelled and toasted)
1/2 tsp. crushed garlic
salt and pepper to taste
1/2 cup blue cheese crumbles
3 tbl. olive oil
1 1/2 tbl. wine vinegar

Combine all ingredients together in large bowl. Toss with vinegar and oil. Sprinkle with blue cheese. Serve.

Tuna-Broccoli Salad

Serves 6

1/3 cup olive oil
1/3 cup parmesan cheese
1 tbl. lemon juice
1 tbl. lime juice
2 cups chopped fresh broccoli (blanched and cooled)
1 1/2 cups fresh spinach (torn in bite sized pieces)
1/4 cup red cabbage (shredded)
6 oz. water packed tuna (drained)
1 cup chopped tomato
1 tbl. bacon bits
1 tsp. garlic powder
salt and pepper to taste

Toss all ingredients together in large bowl. Serve chilled.

If you really look like the picture on your driver's license, you are definitely not well enough to drive.

Serves 8 (tangy and spicy)

I don't use the timer when I cook .... just the smoke alarm!

Curry Dressing:
3 tbl. white wine
2 tbl. pineapple juice
2 tbl. lemon juice
2 tbl. brown sugar
1 1/2 tbl. curry powder
2 tsp. soy sauce
1/2 tsp. garlic powder
1 tsp. onion powder
2 1/2 cups mayonnaise

Combine all ingredients (except mayonnaise) in glass bowl and stir to dissolve. Add mayonnaise and stir until smooth.

Salad:
2 cups shredded iceberg lettuce
2 cups romaine (torn to bite size)
1 cup snow peas
2 med. green onions (chopped)
1 cup thinly sliced zucchini
1 cup thinly sliced cucumber
1/2 cup chopped cauliflower
1/2 cup chopped broccoli
1 large red bell pepper (halved and thinly sliced)
8 cherry tomatoes (halved)
1/4 cup sliced almonds

Combine all ingredients in large bowl. Toss with enough curry dressing to moisten salad. Serve.

So I'm fat. You're ugly. I can diet.

I'm so far behind I think I'm first.

Country Mayonnaise

Makes 1 1/2 cups

2 egg yolks
1 cup vegetable oil
2 tbl. vinegar
1 tsp. Dijon mustard
pinch of salt
1/4 tsp. sugar

In blender, mix yolks, salt, sugar, mustard, and vinegar. With blender running, SLOWLY add oil. Blend to thicken. Store in refrigerator.

Old-Fashioned Potato Salad

Serves 6

2 lbs. potatoes (peeled, boiled, diced)
2 tbl. minced green onions
4 hard boiled eggs (diced)
1 medium dill pickle (diced)
1 tsp. parsley
1/2 tsp. onion salt
1/2 tsp. cilantro
salt and pepper to taste

Combine ingredients together in large bowl. Toss with 2-3 cups Country Mayonnaise. Chill well. Serve.

Celery-Apple Gelatin Salad

Serves 6

1 sm. package cherry gelatin
1 cup boiling water
1/4 cup red cinnamon candies
1/2 cup hot water
1 cup chopped apples (unpeeled)
1 cup chopped celery
1/2 cup walnuts

Dissolve gelatin in boiling water. Add candies. Stir to melt candies. Add hot water. Add remaining ingredients and pour into mold. Chill to set. Remove from mold and serve.

Lime-Pineapple Gelatin Salad

Serves 6

1 sm. package lime gelatin
1 cup boiling water
1/2 cup cold water
1/2 cup pineapple juice (drained from canned pineapple)
2 cups crushed canned pineapple (drained)
1 cup shredded carrot
1 cup mayonnaise
1/4 cup milk

Dissolve gelatin in boiling water. Add cold water and pineapple juice. Pour into mold. Add pineapple and carrot. Stir gently to blend. Chill to set. Remove from mold. Mix together mayonnaise and milk until smooth. Pour over gelatin. Serve.

Orange-Walnut Cream Gelatin Salad

Serves 6

1 sm. package orange gelatin
1 cup boiling water
1/2 cup orange juice
1/2 cup apricot nectar
1 cup whipping cream
1/2 cup chopped walnuts
1/2 cup raisins

Dissolve gelatin in boiling water. Add raisins. Let stand 10 minutes. Add juices. Add walnuts. Whip cream and fold into gelatin mixture. Pour into mold or individual serving cups. Chill to set. Serve.

October 8, 1946

Dear Hannah,

I always new you were quite mad, but this time I'm sure you have totally lost your mind. Tell me it isn't true! You have sold the ranch and opened a pastry shop in town! Hannah, how could you? What do you know about running a business? Contrary to popular belief, Hannah, you are not 20 years of age any more! Didn't anyone bother to tell you that you are an old lady? Doing business and showing a profit do not easily go hand in hand. Honestly, Hannah, what next?

I will admit that you have always been a wizard in the kitchen and that you can squeeze a penny into submission better than anyone I know..... but a pastry shop!?! Well at least you sound happy, which is an unimaginable relief since Andrew's death. In fact you sound more than happy. You sound enthused, energetic and ambitious! Don't tell me you are actually having fun at this?

I really worried that when Patrick and Annie married, and you were forced to live alone for the first time in your entire life, that it would be the end of you. I should have learned not to underestimate you a long time ago.

Well, my dear. Good luck and best wishes to your "Huckleberry Hannah's Homemade Pastries". I know you will be a tremendous success! You exhaust me!
Love, Em

Strawberry-Banana Gelatin Parfaits

Serves 8

1 lg. package strawberry gelatin
1 cup boiling water
2 cups lemon-lime soda (very cold)
1/2 cup juice from cherries
1/2 cup halved maraschino cherries
4 thinly sliced bananas
2 cups whipped cream
8 whole strawberries
nutmeg

Dissolve gelatin in boiling water. Add cherry juice. Add soda slowly (careful, may fizz). Divide sliced bananas and cherries evenly into tall parfait glasses. Pour in gelatin dividing evenly into all 8 glasses. Chill to set. Top with whipped cream. Sprinkle with a pinch of nutmeg. Garnish with whole strawberry.

Garden Salsa

Makes 4 cups (tangy and spicy)

1 cup fresh cilantro
1 large garlic clove
1 medium jalapeno pepper
15 small radishes
4 oz. red onion
6 oz. red bell pepper (cored)
6 oz. tomatoes
2 tbl. olive oil
2 tsp. lemon juice
1/2 tsp. salt

Place all ingredients in food processor and chop fine. Let mixture stand 1 hour in refrigerator. Serve with chips or use lightly on sandwiches.

I gave up smoking, drinking and sex. It was the worst hour of my life.

Fresh Herb Cheese Spread

Makes 2 cups

8 oz. softened cream cheese
4 oz. ricotta cheese
4 oz. sour cream
1 tbl. olive oil
2 tbl. Dijon mustard
1 tbl. lemon juice
3 tbl. basil
3 tbl. dill
2 tbl. parsley
1 tsp. Italian seasoning
1/8 tsp. pepper
1/8 tsp. cayenne pepper
1/8 tsp. salt

Cream cheeses, sour cream, and olive oil. Add remaining ingredients and stir to blend. Store in covered container. Chill.

Cheesy Onion-Olive Spread

Makes 2 cups

1 cup cottage cheese
3 oz. cream cheese (softened)
1/3 cup minced onion
4 oz. chopped black olives
1 garlic clove minced

Mix cheeses together and blend. Add remaining ingredients and stir to blend. Store in covered container. Chill.

One way to save face is to keep the lower half shut.

When you are over the hill you pick up speed.

White Radish Chutney

Makes 1 cup

1/2 cup walnuts (chopped and toasted)
1 cup sliced white radishes
1 small hot green chili
1/2 tsp. salt
1 tsp. cider vinegar

Coarsely puree all ingredients. Store in covered container. Chill.

Green Tomato Chutney

Makes 5 cups

2 lbs. green tomatoes
1/2 lb. tart green apples
1/2 lb. onions
1/2 lb. raisins
1/2 tsp. salt
1/4 tsp. red pepper
1/2 tbl. dry mustard
1 small piece (1/2 inch) fresh ginger
2 cups malt vinegar
1/2 lb. light brown sugar

Coarsely chop tomatoes, apples, onions, and raisins. Tie mustard and ginger in cheesecloth and place in large pot with vegetables. Dissolve sugar in vinegar and pour mixture into pot. Add salt and pepper. Simmer mixture 90 minutes or until thick and spreadable. Discard cheesecloth bag. Serve fresh and store remainder in refrigerator or can mixture in pint jars for later use.

The cost of living is high, but consider the alternatives.

March 22, 1947
Dear Emily,

Oh, Em. Don't worry about me. You know I had to sell the ranch. Who would work it? All the children are gone and have their own lives. I offered it to Patrick, but you know Pat ..... he's no rancher. So the only sensible thing to do was sell. Of course it wasn't easy! I raised seven children on that ranch ...... not to mention myself. But everything has its purpose, and everyone has their day. I was able to walk away from that ranch with no regrets. Now it's time for something new.

Emily, it's been a big adjustment. Living in town is something I have never done, and small town gossip drives me absolutely mad, but I'm getting used to it. I get out of bed every day with a smile on my face and purpose in my heart. I am 61 years old and I'm not getting any younger, so I have to make

Montana Ploughman's Platter

Serves 6

24 lettuce leaves
1 lb. sharp cheddar cheese (chunked)
1 lb. swiss cheese (sliced thin)
1 large loaf sourdough bread (thick sliced)
10 sour dill pickles
10 sweet pickles
1 white onion (thin sliced)
2 large ripe tomatoes (thin sliced)
12 cucumber and radish slices to garnish
large crock Green Tomato Chutney

Arrange all ingredients on large platter. Serve at room temperature.

Sloppy Jose's

Serves 8

2 lbs. lean ground beef
2 tbl. vegetable oil
1 small can chopped green chilies
1/2 cup chopped celery
1 chopped spanish onion
1 large bell pepper (seeded and chopped)
2 cloves garlic (finely chopped)
2 tbl. chili powder
16 oz. stewed tomatoes
2 tbl. dark molasses
1 tbl. paprika
1 tsp. cumin
1 tsp. cilantro
1 tsp. salt
1/4 tsp. pepper

Volunteer workers are good for nothing.

every day count. That is why I decided to open the pastry shop. Huckleberry Hannah's Homemade Pastries was just the ticket to make me tick. I love it.

It's just the cutest little shop. Only 8 tables with blue and white checked table cloths and white dishes decorated with tiny blue cornflowers. I write the menu on a big black board. The soup of the day is whatever I feel like making and the pastries are made fresh every day. I have a big kitchen to stir around in and a front porch with a swing just so I can think of you when I have a few spare moments. That front porch is a pretty popular place! I get lots of company. All the old foggies, like me, come around about 10:00 in the morning for coffee and a sugar puff or a danish roll. Then at noon I get all the "regulars" for soup and sandwich. And at 3:00 the school kids come by to

Sloppy Jose's (cont.)

In large pot brown beef in oil with onions and garlic. Drain excess oil. Add celery, chilies, bell pepper and tomatoes. Stir to blend. Add remaining ingredients and simmer 30 minutes uncovered. Mixture should be thick, but not dry. Add enough water to reach desired consistancy. Serve over halved and buttered South of the Border Corn Muffins.

Cheddar Bacon Pimento Sandwiches

Serves 6

3 cups sharp cheddar cheese (shredded)
18 bacon slices (cooked and crumbled)
4 oz. jar pimentos (drained)
4 green onions (chopped)
1/2 cup mayonnaise
salt, pepper, and garlic powder to taste
6 large french bread rolls or sourdough rolls

Cut rolls in half and spread with mayonnaise. Fill in layers: cheese, bacon, onion, pimento, seasonings. Wrap in foil and heat in 350 degree oven for 15 minutes or until cheese melts. Serve hot with Easy Mushroom Soup.

Toasted Mushroom Sandwiches

Serves 8

2 tbl. butter
1 lb. mushrooms (chopped)
1/4 cup white wine
1 tsp. minced onion
1 cup sour cream
1/4 tsp. garlic powder
1/4 tsp. thyme
1/4 tsp. lemon juice
salt and pepper to taste
16 rye bread slices

visit, have a soda, and gobble up all the broken cookies that I can't sell. (I have been known to break a few extra cookies around 2:30 just so I don't run out.) I usually close the shop around 5:00, but nobody seems to notice, and almost every evening I'll have a few folks looking for a quiet place to sip a little tea and chew a little fat. And every body under the age of thirty calls me "grandma"!

The shop is actually an old house that serves as my home too. I have the entire upper floor to myself. It's warm and sunny and really quite roomy .... more than enough space. I have adopted a fat, lazy calico cat (or she adopted me) that I named Eleanor. A real character that cat. During the day she lounges on the porch and trys to act bored with all the goings on. She never pays any attention to anyone "adult", but around 2:00

Simmer onion, mushrooms, and spices in wine and butter for 20 minutes or until liquid evaporates. Add sour cream and lemon juice. Stir to blend. Butter bread and place 8 slices (butter sides down) onto medium hot skillet. Spoon on mushroom filling. Place remaining bread slices on top (butter sides up). Brown both sides of sandwich. Serve hot.

Reuben Salad Sandwich

Serves 4

3/4 lb. corned beef (thinly sliced)
1 tomato (diced)
1 cup sauerkraut (drained)
1 small onion (sliced)
1/2 tsp. garlic powder
1 tsp. parsely
1/2 cup Italian dressing
1 cup shredded lettuce
1 cup shredded swiss cheese
8 rye bread slices (toasted)
mustard and mayonnaise

Combine corned beef, tomato, sauerkraut, onion, spices and dressing. Chill one hour. Drain. Add lettuce and toss. Spread toast with mustard and mayonnaise. Sprinkle with cheese. Broil until cheese melts. Top 4 slices with corned beef mixture. Top with remaining toast slices. Serve.

Fried Cheese Sticks

Makes 30

1 lb. sharp cheddar cheese (2 x 1 inch sticks)
1 cup warm milk
1/2 cup flour
1/2 tsp. salt
dash pepper
2 eggs (beaten)
1 cup bread crumbs

Combine flour, salt and pepper. Dip cheese in milk. Roll in flour. Roll in egg. Roll in bread crumbs. Fry in very hot oil until golden. Drain. Serve warm.

ICE CREAM SUNDAES & DRINKS

ICE CREAM TALK

Homemade ice cream is a must for any family get-together or special occasion. Everybody loves ice cream so treat your guests to rich creamy ice cream treats. Ice cream is best if the custard base is completely cool before processing the finished product. Store ice cream in tightly covered containers in freezer. Dip ice cream scoop in warm water before use to prevent ice cream from sticking.

BEVERAGE TALK

Unique, tasty beverages are always a big hit even if the only guest is yourself. Hot or cold specialty drinks are refreshing and/or soothing depending on your mood. Don't forget to try the smoothies...Wow!

in the afternoon she perches herself on the porch railing and waits for the children to stop by. What a funny little creature. I enjoy her and she is good company.

So you see, my dear sweet Emily, I'm just fine. Granted there are times late at night that I reach for Andrew in my sleep and remember with a pain in my heart that he isn't there any more. And there are times when I wish there was someone to talk to first thing in the morning, but all in all, I'm happy.

Patrick and Annie come by every Sunday and spend the day. Clare and Bob stop in a couple times a week when they come to town. Mary Ella and Stewart are in town twice a month, at least, and they always stay overnight with me. We laugh and stay up too late telling hilarious stories on each other and all other innocent, defense-less victims who happen to deserve to be picked on.

Hannah's Heavenly Hot Fudge Sauce

Makes 2 cups (to die for!)

3/4 cup butter
6 squares unsweetened chocolate
3 1/2 cups sugar
1/4 tsp. salt
2 cups evaporated milk
1 tsp. vanilla

Melt butter and chocolate in double boiler. Stir in sugar 1/2 cup at a time. Blend well (mixture will be thick and dry). Add salt. Slowly stir in milk, 1/4 cup at a time. Continue to cook over low heat, stirring constantly for 8-10 minutes to blend flavors and dissolve ingredients. Do not allow to boil. Remove from heat and add vanilla. Serve hot or cold. Store in refrigerator.

Bittersweet Chocolate Sauce

Makes 1 cup (especially for chocolate purists)

10 oz. semi-sweet chocolate (finely chopped)
2/3 cup evaporated milk
1/2 tsp. vanilla
1/2 tsp. butter

Melt chocolate in double boiler. Slowly add 1/3 cup milk stirring constantly. Thin with remaining milk if needed. Remove from heat. Add vanilla and butter. Stir to blend. Store in refrigerator. Serve warm or cold.

When in doubt . . . mumble.

Then of course, all the grandchildren end up here, at one time or another, in the "after school broken cookie bunch".

My life is full .... Praise the Lord. And when I have a weak or teary moment he's right there to take my hand and help me through it.

So don't worry. You are right about one thing though, Em. I am a terrible bookkeeper.

My love to all. "Huckleberry Hannah" (a.k.a "grandma")

Emily's Peanut Butter Chocolate Sauce
Makes 1 cup

5 1/2 oz. evaporated milk
1/2 cup sugar
2 squares unsweetened chocolate (chopped)
1 tbl. butter
1 1/2 tbl. creamy peanut butter
dash almond extract

Combine milk, sugar, chocolate and peanut butter in double boiler. Simmer to melt ingredients together. When well blended, add butter and extract. Serve warm. Store in refrigerator.

Variation: For Mocha Sauce, substitute peanut butter with 3 tsp. instant coffee, and almond extract with vanilla. Yummy!

Creamy Caramel Sauce
Makes 1 cup

1 cup sugar
1/8 tsp. lemon juice
3/4 cup whipping cream

Melt 1/4 cup sugar in double boiler stirring constantly. Add remaining sugar, 1/4 cup at a time, stirring each addition until thoroughly melted. Add lemon juice and stir until syrup is golden brown. Bring cream to boil and add gradually to sugar mixture stirring until smooth. Store in refrigerator. Serve warm.

I'm so broke I can't even afford to pay attention.

Always wash your hands before meals, that way you can get a better grip on your food.

Maple Walnut Sauce

Makes 1 1/4 cups

1/2 cup chopped and toasted walnuts
1 cup maple syrup
2 tsp. rum flavoring
1 tsp. lemon juice

Warm syrup on low heat. Mix in nuts, flavoring, and juice. Blend together. Store in refrigerator. Serve warm or cold.

Mocha-Cinnamon Sundae

6 servings

Chocolate-Cinnamon Ice Cream:
2 cups half and half
2 cups whipping cream
4 cinnamon sticks
12 oz. semi-sweet chocolate (chopped)
2 oz.unsweetened chocolate (chopped)
1 1/2 tsp. ground cinnamon
8 egg yolks
1 cup brown sugar
1 tsp. instant coffee
pinch of salt

Scald half and half with cinnamon sticks. Let stand 15 minutes. Remove cinnamon Sticks. Melt both chocolates and instant coffee with whipping cream in double boiler, stirring until smooth. Remove from heat. Beat yolks and sugar. Gradually add half and half mixture to egg mixture, stirring constantly. Return to heat and thicken. Do not boil. Gradually add chocolate mixture. Blend. Chill. Process in ice cream maker. Freeze.

Middle age: When a broad mind and a narrow waist change places .

Never loan money to a friend... it ruins their memory.

Caramel-Coffee Sauce:
1 cup sugar
3 tbl. water
3/4 cup whipping cream
4 tsp. instant coffee (dissolved in 1/4 cup hot water)
1 tsp. vanilla

Cook sugar and water over low heat until sugar dissolves. Increase heat and boil until mixture turns caramel color. Remove from heat and gradually add cream (carefull, may spatter). Stir vigorously. Add coffee and boil one minute. Remove from heat. Add vanilla. Serve lukewarm over ice cream. Garnish with whipped cream.

Strawberry-Chocolate Chunk Sundae

Makes 6 servings

Chocolate Chunk Ice Cream:
4 1/3 cups half and half
1 cup sugar
6 egg yolks
1/4 tsp. ground ginger
1 1/2 tsp. vanilla
8 oz. semi-sweet chocolate chips

Scald half and half with sugar until sugar dissolves. Beat yolks. Gradually add half and half to eggs, stirring constantly. Add ginger and vanilla. Cool. Add chocolate chips and process in ice cream maker. Freeze.

Chocolate Strawberry Sauce:
8 oz. semi-sweet chocolate (chopped)
3/4 cup water
1/4 cup sugar
1/8 tsp. ground cinnamon
3 tbl. butter
1/2 tsp. instant coffee
1 cup frozen stawberries (thawed and pureed)

June 9, 1947

Dear Hannah,
    Franklin slipped away quietly in his sleep yesterday morning. It happened just the way he wanted it to. I came in to bring his breakfast and knew he was gone. I sat next to him and held his hand for a few minutes. No tears... I shed those years ago when I knew I would lose him. So this morning, with the sun filtering in onto his peaceful face, the only thing I could say was "God's speed, my love....God's speed."
    Last night I sat in the swing and rocked in the moonlight. All the years of Franklin filled me. Years of laughter and music, family and friends, babies, Christmas trees and Thanksgiving dinners surrounded me. I felt so close to him...for a moment, I almost thought I heard

Strawberry Chocolate Chunk Sundae (cont.)

Melt chocolate and sugar. Add instant coffee and cinnamon. Blend. Gradually add water. Simmer but do not boil, stirring constantly. Add strawberries and blend well. Remove from heat. Add butter. Blend. Serve lukewarm over ice cream. Garnish with whipped cream.

Very Berry Sundae

Serves 6

Blackberry Ice cream:
2 1/2 pints fresh or frozen blackberries
2 cups whipping cream
1 cup sugar
4 egg yolks

Puree berries and strain if desired. Scald cream with sugar until sugar dissolves, stirring constantly. Beat yolks. Gradually add hot cream and blend. Return to heat and thicken but do not boil. Stir in berries. Chill. Process in ice cream maker. Freeze.

Boysenberry Sauce:
2 cups frozen boysenberries (pureed and strained)
1/3 cup water
1/2 cup sugar
pinch of salt
whipped cream
huckleberries or blueberries

Mix frozen berries, water, sugar, and salt. Boil until reduced to syrupy texture. Cool to lukewarm. Pour over ice cream. Top with whipped cream and huckleberries.

When the going gets tough, the tough go shopping.

119

him whistling. Isn't that funny? The very thing that annoyed me the most for so many years is what I miss. I thought about my childhood....my wonderful childhood. I thought about you and me and all the things we have shared over the years.

Hannah, I want to come home. There is nothing left for me here and suddenly I can't bare to be away from you and Montana one minute longer.

Anyway, Hannah. I was thinking. You are alone. I am alone. Why don't we be two old widows alone together? I could be a big help, you know. After all I'm sure you could use someone with a good head for business right about now.

Write me and tell me what you think of my idea. We belong together. Loving you, Emily

Simple Scrumptious Fruit Sherbets

Makes 1 quart

Basic Sherbet:
1 cup fruit
1/2 cup fruit juice
2 tbl. honey
4 tsp. lemon or lime juice
1 egg white (room temp.)

Combine fruit, juice, honey, and lemon juice in blender and puree. Beat egg white to soft peak. Fold in fruit mixture. Cover and freeze.

Sherbet Fruit Combination Ideas:

Mango Fruit with Orange Juice
Apple Fruit with Cranberry Juice
Boysenberry Fruit with Apricot Juice
Orange Fruit with Mint Juice
Peach Fruit with Champagne
Strawberry Fruit with Pineapple Juice

THE LIST IS ENDLESS!

Chocolate Mousse Ice Cream

Makes about 2 quarts (incredibly smooth!)

3/4 cup sugar
1/4 cup diluted evaporated milk
1/2 cup water
16 oz. semi-sweet chocolate (chopped)
6 egg yolks
1 quart whipping cream (whipped)

Heat sugar, milk, and water over low heat until sugar dissolves. Cook over medium heat. Boil 3 minutes. Remove from heat and gradually add chocolate. Stir to smooth. Cool . Beat yolks and add to chocolate mixture. Stir to blend. Gently fold in cream to chocolate mixture. Process in ice cream maker. Freeze.

Serve with Hot Fudge Sauce or fresh fruit.

P.S. Maybe we could call the shop Hannah's Homemade Pastries and Emily's English Tea Room?

Chunky Chocolate-Raspberry Ice Cream

Makes about 1 quart (yummy and creamy)

1/2 cup sugar
1/2 cup water
5 egg yolks
10 oz. semi-sweet chocolate (melted & cooled)
1 cup fresh or frozen raspberries (chopped)
1 1/2 cups whipping cream (whipped)

Heat sugar and water until sugar dissolves. Increase heat and bring to boil. Beat yolks until pale. Slowly beat in hot syrup. Return mixture to pan and heat over low heat until mixture thickens (3-4 minutes). Do not boil. Refrigerate over night or until mixture is completely cool. Fold in raspberries, chocolate and cream and process in ice cream maker. Freeze to firm.

White Chocolate Ice Cream

Makes 2 quarts

1 1/2 cups half and half or evaporated milk
16 oz. white chocolate (chopped)
4 eggs
1 1/2 cups sugar
2 1/2 cups whipping cream

Scald half and half (use a double boiler if you have one). Add chocolate. Reduce heat to simmer and cook until chocolate melts. Remove from heat. Beat eggs with mixer. Add sugar and beat until dissolved. Slowly add chocolate mixture, stirring constantly. Beat in cream and refrigerate until cool. Process in ice cream maker. Freeze.

Are you married? No, I was hit by a car.

Chocolate-Cherry-Coconut Ice Cream

Makes 1 1/2 quarts

1/3 cup coconut cream
5 egg yolks
1/2 cup sugar
1 cup coarsely chopped, pitted, fresh or frozen cherries
2 tbl. water
1 tsp. coconut extract
1/2 tsp. rum extract
1 1/4 cups whipping cream (whipped)
6 oz. semi-sweet chocolate (coarsely grated)
1/4 cup flaked coconut

Simmer coconut cream. Beat yolks and sugar until pale. Gradually beat hot coconut mixture into egg mixture. Return to heat and thicken, stirring constantly (about 4 minutes). Cool and chill. Simmer cherries and water until cherries are tender and water is nearly evaporated. Cool. Add extracts. Fold cherry mixture and whipping cream into custard. Process in ice cream maker. When nearly firm, add chocolate and coconut. Freeze.

Definition of picnic: A meadow lark.

Chocolate-Nutty Caramel Ice Cream

Makes 2 quarts

Do unto others before they do unto you.

Caramel:
1 1/3 cups sugar
10 tbl. water
1 1/3 cups whipping cream

Cook sugar and water over low heat until sugar dissolves. Increase heat and boil until mixture turns golden brown, (about 30 minutes) stirring constantly. Slowly pour in 1 1/3 cups whipping cream (be careful, may spatter). Blend well. Cool.

Ice Cream:
2 cups evaporated milk (diluted)
5 egg yolks
1/2 cups sugar
1 cup whipping cream (whipped)
6 oz. semi-sweet chocolate (coarsely grated)
3/4 cup coarsely chopped salted peanuts

Beat eggs and 1/3 cup sugar until pale. Slowly beat hot milk into egg mixture. Return to heat and thicken, stirring constantly. Do not boil. Cool. Fold in whipping cream and caramel. Process in ice cream maker. When nearly firm add chocolate and peanuts. Freeze.

Rum Raisin Ice Cream

Ice cream maker not necessary for this one!

Makes about 1 1/2 quarts

1 1/2 cups half and half
2 tsp. rum extract
3/4 cup sugar
1/4 cup flour
1/4 tsp. salt
2 eggs
2 cups whipping cream
2 tsp. vanilla
1/2 cup raisins

Scald half and half and raisins. Combine flour, sugar, and salt. Gradually blend in milk mixture. Cook over low heat stirring constantly until thickened. Beat eggs until pale. Slowly add to milk mixture, stirring constantly. Return to heat again and stir to thicken. Cover and chill. Add cream, vanilla, coconut, and rum extract. Beat with electric mixer until frothy. Pour into shallow bowl and freeze.

Creamy Vanilla Ice Cream

Makes 2 quarts

2 cups milk
4 cups whipping cream
1 vanilla bean (split)
2 cups sugar
12 egg yolks

Scald milk and 1 1/2 cups cream with vanilla bean. Remove from heat. Scrape seeds from vanilla bean into mixture; return bean. Let steep 10 mintues. Remove bean and discard. Add 1 cup sugar to milk mixture. Bring to boil stirring constantly. Beat yolks and remaining sugar until pale. Gradually beat in hot cream mixture. Return to heat and stir to thicken. Do not boil. Cover and chill. Process in ice cream maker. Freeze.

Peanut Butter Ice Cream

Makes 1 1/2 quarts

3 1/2 cups half and half
9 egg yolks
1 cup sugar
1 tsp. vanilla
pinch of salt
1/2 cup whipping cream
1 cup chunky peanut butter

September 21, 1947
Dear Emily,

Bless your dear old heart! Of course you can come home! You're right, we DO need each other. You're right too, that we would be a great team. "Emily's English Tea Room" is a bit much, but we can work that out when you get here. A better name might be .... "The Aging Filly"!

Oh, Em, if you hurry you can be home for the holidays and I promise a white Christmas made to order just for you. We can go out carolling on Christmas Eve just like we did when we were kids. We can make popcorn and cranberry strings for the tree. And we can sit around and lie about our age all you want. So hurry up and pack up! I can't believe you are really coming home at last.

Emily! I just had a terrible thought! What if we can't recognize each other at the train station. I'm not even going to try and described myself. Tell you what. Just step off that train and look for a chubby, gray haired, old lady gliding across the platform with a yellow rose in her teeth!

*See you soon!
Missing you, Hannah*

Peanut Butter Ice Cream (cont.)

Scald half and half and peanut butter until peanut butter is dissolved. Beat yolks, sugar, vanilla and salt until pale . Gradually add half and half mixture, stirring constantly. Return to heat and thicken (continue to stir). Do not boil. Blend in cream. Chill. Process in ice cream maker. Freeze.

Fresh Fruit Ice Cream

Makes 2 quarts

This is a wonderful recipe to be used with ANY fresh fruit. Just follow the basic recipe and add 2 cups mashed fruit. My favorites are peach, nectarine, banana or raspberry. OR get creative and use any 2 cup combination you choose.

1 1/2 cups sugar
1 cup water
2 cups mashed fruit
2 tsp. lemon juice
1 quart whipping cream

Heat sugar and water until sugar dissolves. Increase heat and simmer gently five minutes. Do not stir. Cool completely. Add lemon juice to fruit and blend (you can puree fruit if you like a smoother ice cream). Mix in cream and cooled syrup. Cover and chill. Process in ice cream maker.

Fresh Fruit Smoothies

These are wonderfully refreshing treats perfect for any time of year.
Makes one serving

1 cup Fresh Fruit Ice Cream
1 cup lime or fruit soda OR fruit juice
1 tsp. vanilla
1/4 tsp. almond extract

Blend and enjoy!

Auntie Ruth's Fruit Punch

(a delicious hit for any party)

A bachelor's definition of gourmet: Anything above room temperature.

2 large packets cherry sweetened drink powder
2 large packets orange sweetened drink powder
1 48 oz. can pineapple juice
1 large bottle of ginger ale
4 mashed bananas
4 cups sugar
48 oz. water

Mix all ingredients together (except bananas and ginger ale). Fill 4 ice cube trays with punch mixture and freeze. Chill remaining punch. When ready to serve add frozen punch cubes, bananas, and ginger ale and stir to blend. Serve in large punch bowl.

Blackberry-Mint Tea Punch

Makes 2 quarts

12 cups cold water
10 blackberry herb tea bags
10 orange spice herb tea bags
5 black tea bags
2/3 cup crushed mint leaves
1/2 cup honey
1/2 cup lemon juice
fresh mint sprigs
lemon slices

Combine water, crushed mint, and tea bags in large covered container. Let stand in window for at least 12 hours. Heat 1 cup of tea mixture and honey until honey dissolves. Add heated tea to remaining tea. Strain. Blend in lemon juice. Fill 3 ice cube trays with tea and freeze. Chill remaining punch. Place frozen tea cubes in tall glasses. Cover with punch. Garnish with lemon slices and mint sprigs.

Apricot-Peach Punch

Makes 2 1/2 quarts

Time wounds all heels.

2 lbs. frozen unsweetened sliced peaches.
1 12-oz. can apricot juice
1/4 cup lime juice
1/4 tsp. almond extract
1 large bottle chilled ginger ale
5 lemon slices
5 lime slices
5 orange slices

Puree peaches and apricot juice in blender. Add lime juice and extract. Blend. Pour into punch bowl. Add ginger ale. Stir to blend. Float fruit slices on top.

Pineapple Juleps

Makes 8 servings

1 small pineapple trimmed or 16 oz. canned pineapple with juice
4 cups ice cubes
1/2 cup fresh mint
1/2 cup sugar
1/2 tsp. rum flavoring
1/2 tsp. almond flavoring
2 tbl. lime juice
several fresh mint leaves

Puree pineapple and fresh mint in blender. Add sugar. Blend and taste (add more sugar if desired). Add ice cubes. Blend. Add flavoring and lime juice. Serve in tall glasses over ice and garnish with fresh mint leaves.

I hate intolerant people.

Epilogue

Emily did indeed return home to her beloved Montana just as the country geared up to the "post war" economic boom.

Huckleberry Hannah's Homemade Pastries, under the clever management of Emily and the creative cookery of Hannah, grew by leaps and bounds. Soon the tiny shop was providing bread to nearly every home in the area. Pastries from "Hannah's" were on the menu of every restaurant and cafe. And, Hannah's Homemade Cookies became a household "buzz word" in the 1950's.

The whole town loved the two women, and Hannnah and Emily were rich with family and friends.

Emily quickly became the practical side of this very special pair, while Hannah was ... "just Hannah".... convinced that every day should contain, at least, one hearty laugh.

The two women picked up their childhood friendship without missing a step. They were certainly never bored, and lived full and active lives late into their eighties. (I wonder if Hannah ever knew about Emily's diary.)

Sparkling Apple Splash

Makes 2 quarts

2 medium oranges
2 medium lemons
1/4 cup sugar
1/4 tsp. cinnamon
pinch of allspice
6-oz. can frozen apple juice
4 cups apple cider
2 cups sparkling water

Peel 1 orange, squeeze and reserve juice. Cut second orange into thin slices. Squeeze and reserve juice from 1 lemon. Cut second lemon into thin slices. Place orange and lemon slices into bottom of large pitcher. Sprinkle with sugar and spices. Add remaining ingredients. Stir. Serve over ice in tall or stemmed glasses.

Banana-Coconut Slush

Makes 1 quart

3 bananas
3 tbl. lemon juice
1 orange
6 oz. can sweetened coconut cream
6 oz. can frozen pink lemonade
crushed ice
thin lime slices

Peel, chunk, wrap in plastic wrap, and freeze bananas and orange. Puree frozen fruit with coconut cream and lemonade. Pour over crushed ice in wide mouthed glasses and garnish with lime slices.

People who predict earthquakes are fault finders.

Hannah's Pitcher Perfect Lemonade

Makes 2 1/2 quarts

1 cup sugar
1 cup water
1 1/3 cups fresh lemon juice
grated rind from 4 lemons
2 quarts cold water

Boil water and sugar until sugar is completely dissolved. Cool. Add lemon juice and rind. Pour into large pitcher. Chill. Serve over ice with slices of lemon garnish.

You know it's going to be a bad day when your twin sister forgets your birthday.

Strawberry Yogurt Shake

Makes 3 cups

1 cup cold milk
1 can orange soda
1 cup frozen strawberries
1 cup strawberry yogurt
1 tbl. lemon juice
1 tbl. vanilla
1 tbl. honey

Combine soda, strawberries, and yogurt in blender. Puree. Add remaining ingredients. Blend again. Pour into large glasses. (For a terrific protein blast, add 8 oz. soft tofu. Blend well.)

Cantaloupe-Ginger Spritzer

Makes 2 cups

1 cup chopped cantaloupe
1 cup orange juice
1 1/2 tsp. ginger
1 can lemon-lime soda
6 ice cubes

Cantaloupe-Ginger Spritzer (cont.)

Combine all ingredients in blender. Puree. Serve in tall glasses. Garnish with lime wedge if desired.

Where does virgin wool come from? From sheep that run the fastest.

Huckleberry-Peach Cooler

Makes 3 cups

1 cup frozen sliced peaches
1 1/2 cups fresh or frozen huckleberries or blueberries
1 cup cold milk
1 cup vanilla yogurt
1 tsp. cinnamon
1/2 tsp. nutmeg
1 tbl. honey

Combine peaches, berries, and milk in blender. Puree. Add remaining ingredients. Blend. Serve in tall glasses. Garnish with a pinch of cinnamon.

Blueberry-Watermelon Quencher

Makes 2 cups

1 cup chopped watermelon (remove all seeds)
1 cup frozen blueberries
1 cup cranberry juice cocktail

Combine all ingredients in blender. Puree. Serve in tall glasses.

Granny's Hot Cocoa Mix

Makes 1 dry gallon (so convenient, and oh so good)

1 quart dry powdered milk
2 cups dry instant creamer
16 oz. dry chocolate milk mix
2 cups powdered sugar
(For mocha flavored mix: Add 1 small jar of instant coffee.)

Mix all ingredients in gallon glass or plastic jar with lid. Store in dry place.

To reconstitute: Spoon 1/3 cup mix into coffee mug. Fill mug half full with boiling water. Stir to dissolve. Fill mug with hot water. Stir and drink. Garnish with tiny marshmallows or cinnamon stick.

Cuisine: Any food you can't pronounce.

Hot Buttered Country Cider

Makes 2 quarts

2 quarts apple cider
2/3 cup dried apple slices
2 tbl. golden raisins
1/4 tsp. ground cloves
1 cinnamon stick (broken into pieces)
2 tbl. lemon juice
1/4 stick chilled butter
extra long cinnamon sticks

Simmer first 5 ingredients covered for 15 minutes. Remove from heat and add lemon juice. Ladle into mugs. Garnish with pat of butter and cinnamon stick.

Citrus Toddy for Your Body

makes 1 quart (head to toe warmer)

2 1/2 quarts water
5 cloves
1/2 cup honey
1 cup orange juice
8 tbl. lemon juice
1/4 cup lime juice

Simmer water and cloves for 10 minutes. Add honey. Simmer 1 minute. Add juices. Serve hot with floating lemon or lime slices.

If everything is coming your way, you are in the wrong lane.

Old-fashioned Orange Cranberry Warmer

makes 2 quarts

1 cup orange juice
6 cups water
20 cloves
1 cinnamon stick
12 oz. frozen cranberry juice
1/2 cup golden raisins
1/2 tsp. cardamon
3 tbl. lemon juice
orange slices

Simmer all ingredients (except orange slices and cardamon) for 10 minutes. Stir in cardamon. Ladle into mugs. Garnish with orange slices.

A woman's place is in the home, and she should go there directly from work.

Category Index

Category Index

Category Index

ABOUT THE AUTHOR

Deanna Hansen-Doying has owned and operated businesses since the age of 20, and has been a marketing consultant for the past 10 years. Her hobby is collecting and developing wonderful recipes, cooking, baking and taking the research for this book off her waistline. Now semi-retired, she lives on a ranch near Eureka, Montana with 4 horses, 3 cats, 2 dogs, and one husband (not necessarily in that order), where she is currently writing the next book in the Huckleberry Hannah Series.

ABOUT THE ARTIST

Tim Acosta currently resides in Pueblo, Colorado, and is an award winning graphic artist. Known for his unique style of design and caricature art, Tim has become, "the man to see" for the best in publication illustrations.

A Great Gift Idea!

Please send me:_____copies of HUCKLEBERRY HANNAH'S
COUNTRY COOKING SAMPLER.

I have enclosed $12.95 per book plus $2.00 shipping and handling per copy.
Enclosed $_____

Name_____

Address_____

City_____State_____Zip_____

Make checks payable to: MONTANA COUNTRY SAMPLERS,
BOX 664, EUREKA, MT. 59917

*Allow 3-4 weeks for delivery
*Canadian orders: Please pay in U.S. funds and allow an additional $.50 for shipping.

Please send me_____copies of HUCKLEBERRY HANNAH'S
COUNTRY COOKING SAMPLER.

I have enclosed $12.95 per book plus $2.00 for shipping and handling
per copy. Enclosed $_____

Name_____

Address_____

City_____State_____Zip_____

Make checks payable to: MONTANA COUNTRY SAMPLERS,
BOX 664, EUREKA, MT 59917

*Allow 3-4 weeks for delivery
*Canadian orders please pay in U.S. funds and allow an additional $.50 for shipping.

YES, I would like my name to be placed on the MONTANA COUNTRY
SAMPLERS mailing list!

Name_____

Address_____

City_____State_____Zip_____